M000198307

Also by Martha McPhee

Bright Angel Time

Gorgeous Lies

L'America

Dear Money

An Elegant Woman

Omega
Farm

A Memoir

Martha McPhee

SCRIBNER

New York   London   Toronto   Sydney   New Delhi

Scribner
An Imprint of Simon & Schuster, Inc.
1230 Avenue of the Americas
New York, NY 10020

Copyright © 2023 by Martha McPhee

All rights reserved, including the right to reproduce this book or portions thereof
in any form whatsoever. For information, address Scribner Subsidiary Rights
Department, 1230 Avenue of the Americas, New York, NY 10020.

First Scribner hardcover edition September 2023

SCRIBNER and design are registered trademarks of The Gale Group, Inc., used under
license by Simon & Schuster, Inc., the publisher of this work.

For information about special discounts for bulk purchases, please contact Simon &
Schuster Special Sales at 1-866-506-1949 or business@simonandschuster.com.

The Simon & Schuster Speakers Bureau can bring authors to your live event. For more
information or to book an event, contact the Simon & Schuster Speakers Bureau at
1-866-248-3049 or visit our website at www.simonspeakers.com.

Interior design by Jaime Putorti

Photographs on pp. 1 and 107 by Pryde Brown

Manufactured in the United States of America

1   3   5   7   9   10   8   6   4   2

Library of Congress Cataloging-in-Publication Data has been applied for.

ISBN 978-1-9821-9799-5
ISBN 978-1-9821-9801-5 (ebook)

For Livia and Jasper

Part One

The night before I left, my mother slept in bed with me. She was afraid to sleep alone. I awoke to her reaching for me with her left hand, the one that shook involuntarily with what doctors call an essential tremor, as if the tremor were a necessary thing. In the dark room, far past midnight, the tremor rustling the sheets and my arm, I felt the familiar, overwhelming frustration that could clobber me no matter how hard I tried for it not to. Her shaking hand, gripping my arm, her desperate need to feel that I was there. I hated it. The need. The fear. That she was gone already, a ghost beside me in my bed. She had dementia, had had it already for ten years—a slow, steady decline until she couldn't formulate sentences, had to wear diapers, had accidents, was always anxious to go home, worried about the babies, so worried about the babies. I hated her dementia. I was angry with it. The trembling hand had an urgent grip on me. I grabbed it and held it hard so that it was forced to stop shaking. I hated myself. Gone was my mother. The dementia had replaced her with a quaking, shaking hand. I got up, got her up, and led her down the long hall covered in portraits of us as children, the ten of us, photos my mother had taken herself, to her own room, where I tucked her into her bed and gave her a cold, fast kiss.

I had been with her for a year, sheltering in place with her during the pandemic, in my childhood home. My husband, my daughter, my son, our cat, and our dog had come to her from New York City on March 15, 2020—the pandemic spreading around the globe, a tide of death and destruction whose surging numbers were now, a year later, too big for the mind to take in. Indeed, much about the experience of the pandemic seemed to expose not just the limits of my brain's ability to process the daily scale of death, but to reveal, from the moment we began to isolate by the millions, the early onset of a condition that, because of our individual separateness, didn't have a name, though it did have its own uncanny prefiguration in Gabriel García Márquez's novel *One Hundred Years of Solitude*—the episode in which a village slowly loses its collective mind. The village inhabitants cope by leaving notes for themselves everywhere to guide them through their days, the notes moving from the practical sort you might find in a kitchen to the metaphysical sort ("There is a God"): a set-piece moment of magical realism that came to seem more like cinema verité. The country of my birth was like that village unmoored from memory, like my mother, whose sense of both identity and direction were disappearing in front of me.

In March 2021, I was the last one of my family remaining here in New Jersey. My daughter had returned to college, my son to high school, and my husband to take care of him in our old life in New York City. We had a new president; the country hadn't fallen apart, or not yet, anyway; one hundred million people had been vaccinated, with two hundred million more projected by the coming May. The dismay and bafflement I'd felt, as a pervasive national mood, had been replaced by a wave of relative sanity, determination, damage assessment, and repair to institutions that seemed to depend too much on the presumption that public office holders would act in good faith.

The year had been a disaster for my son, Jasper, a high school junior; he'd resisted every minute of our year in New Jersey and now refused to visit, but he pleaded with me to come home for his spring vacation, to come with him and my husband to visit two of my sisters in Idaho, where one of them had recently moved. People were traveling again. I had gotten vaccinated, along with my husband, so I made plans for Idaho.

I was afraid to leave. It was an abstract fear—one I couldn't quite identify or make sense of, but that I had plenty of excuses for: though my mother had a caregiver named Dayana, here with her son from Colombia, the job was too big for one person alone; we had also begun projects at my mother's, my family and I—the garden, the flock of chickens now full-grown and laying ten eggs a day and needing care; the eradication of a bamboo grove; and the forest. There was a massive restoration project that involved creating an understory; there were invasive species to be removed, native grasses to be seeded, oak and maple saplings to be planted. There was so much fixing still to do. I was afraid that if I left, I would lose all that I'd made and restored in the past year at my childhood home—that it would be taken away, cease to exist, would slip through my fingers and become nothing, that without me my mother would die. As frustrated as I was with her condition, as hard as it was to watch her die incrementally, I felt I was keeping her safe. If she was safe, if she was alive, there was still time to understand what I was doing in New Jersey, what I wanted from the past, and, somehow, to fix all of it: the house, the land, my mother, my childhood. My need to repair and renew was urgent, desperate. My mother had messed up a lot. I couldn't have put it so concretely in the moment, and in that year in New Jersey I often wondered what I was doing there—but I would come to see that my fear of leaving was inextricably bound to my desire to understand what had happened, and to make it better.

My mother too was afraid. I could feel it. She understood something was very wrong with her, but not what. She understood more than we allowed. She understood that I was leaving and it upset her. On the few occasions I had gone away for a night or two, she always pleaded, "Don't go," a haunting in her eyes. "Don't go." Though she struggled to form anything coherent, she could say those two words. What she really meant was anybody's guess, but it kicked up an ambiguity I am almost ashamed to admit to. My mother's métier was to be improvident, making herself vulnerable to the winds of chance, a characteristic that could be endearing but which also meant she had prepared for nothing. It was left to my sisters and me to sort things out, and as I was the one with her, the sorting out fell to me. I too wanted to be taken care of—I wanted her to take care of me—and it was not going to happen. That's what I saw in her terrified eyes, in her quaking hand. Even so, I didn't want to leave. I believed that if I just worked harder, I could fix even this.

But I did leave for Idaho.

We were in our seats, the plane idling on the tarmac waiting to be de-iced. It was six a.m. I leaned my head against the window and felt suddenly the onslaught of a tremendous, overpowering emotion, a vision, as clear as day: my mother appeared before me, my mother as she had once been and as I hadn't seen her in many years. Pryde, named by her own mother for a girl she'd met as a child in the West—a pretty girl who was killed when a horse kicked her in the head. My mother always hated the name. She was there saying goodbye to me some forty years before at this same airport as I was setting off on an adventure to Italy on a summer exchange. She was smiling and so young, my stepfather at her side—both of them excited for what lay ahead for me. There she was returning home late after a day at work, camera bags hanging off her shoulders, tired, but smiling—her beautiful gap-toothed smile, her blond hair. There she was digging up myrtle from deep in the woods behind our old house in Princeton, my three older sisters and I, very young, helping her, placing the up-rooted ground cover with the little blue pinwheel flowers into a child's red wagon to carry home to be transplanted into our garden. There she was alone with me in the kitchen of that same home, my sisters racing down the driveway late to catch the school bus, and how I loved to be alone with her, to have her to myself, hoping my sisters would stay at school forever. I never wanted to leave her side as a little girl. In fact, I refused to go to nursery school and spent the day with her instead at Head Start in town, where she volunteered as a teacher. There she was at Brown's in London for tea, my sisters and me in

7

matching Liberty print dresses she had made herself on the Singer. There she was walking my children to school when they were young, singing to them about lambs and ivy. There she was behind her camera telling me to "Relax your lip, Martha." There she was driving with my sisters and me late into the night in our old beat-up green station wagon, trying to decide if she should leave my stepfather or not. He had a temper, had hit her, had caused her to get stitches and suffer a concussion, but she had a baby with him, still in a crib, our little sister, Joan. There Mom was taking me to Radio City Music Hall for my birthday in June because I wanted to see the Christmas Spectacular. She tried to explain that it was June, but I insisted the Rockettes would be there. I insisted on a Baskin-Robbins ice cream cake, too, that we'd bring home for everyone to share. I refused to believe that it would melt. She bought it anyway and anyway it melted in the car on the drive from New York City to home. There she was stealing daffodils from the yard of an abandoned house. A cop caught her and arrested her, had very little sense of humor as she tried, the way she could with that smile of hers, to flirt her way out of the situation. There she was laughing as my stepfather told the story of her arrest to the dinner table filled with kids, the ten of us—his five, Mom's four, and their one. Then the whole table was laughing at Mom's arrest for stealing the jolly sunny flowers for our yard.

The images didn't stop. They just kept coming. Mom as I hadn't seen her in years, so immersed in the present, so aware of the shedding of herself, piece by piece by piece, the disease eating her alive. I could not stop the tears. My husband looked at me, baffled as the plane lifted off, sympathetic as we sailed across Pennsylvania, confused and then alarmed as we slid through a fog so dense you could see nothing outside the window, consoling as we approached Salt Lake City on the initial descent, holding my hand as we took off again for Hailey. I was careful not to let Jasper see, but I could not stop the tears. I had never cried like this before. Just when I thought the crying was finished a new image of my mother would appear. There she was in her first photography studio in Princeton, New Jersey, with her partner Elaine, both of them pulling back the skin of their cheekbones; "Just one tuck," they would say. There she was in her garden battling the weeds, which didn't seem to understand the word *no*, the persistent chrysanthemum weeds with their endless subterranean root system that her drive and determination and her Japanese sickle would conquer. There she was lying in bed with me as a teenager, afraid that I was pregnant, sobbing against her chest, her hand stroking my head, reassuring me. There she was alive and beautiful and my mother, fully intact and in charge of herself, spoiling my children, decorating the Christmas tree, hanging the Easter eggs from the chandelier, eggs that we had blown and painted ourselves over the years; there she was giving us Advent calendars at Thanksgiving though we were well into our thirties. There she was racing into the city to help with a child's birthday party, to be there at a birth, for a celebration, for anything we needed. Imperfect mother, yes, but there now before me as I raced across the sky, alive, sitting with me on the deck overlooking the vast lawn and the field beyond, sipping a glass of wine with me at dusk as the sun spilled colors across the evening. "Isn't it so beautiful here," she'd always say. There she was.

And then this happened: up there in the sky, the Rockies spreading out as far as I could see, the sun dazzling the snowcapped peaks, I realized that I wasn't afraid that I would lose what I had made across the last year in my childhood home. Rather, now that I had left, I was afraid I might never return home again, that I'd prefer to be Elsewhere, that I'd discover that I didn't care to continue the quest, to do the work, that it was all right to leave the past unresolved. Mothers make mistakes, sometimes really big ones for which there can be no apology.

OMEGA FARM, MY MOTHER'S home, sits on top of a hill, the highest point in Hunterdon County, New Jersey, with sweeping views over fields and farms, the Sourland Mountains unfurling in the distance to meet a big and open sky. When you sit on the deck, which faces north and overlooks the lawn and fields, the sun rises on your right, just beyond a barn and another field and chicken run, a rooster crowing. The sun sets in spectacular fashion across the valley. The midday heat, which comes on hard and thick in July, is cut in half by a canopy of enormous oaks and ash. So complete is the canopy that a satellite image on Google shows only trees—no house. My mother owns that house and the forty-five acres surrounding it, thirty-five of which is forest tumbling south down a hill to a creek along which run trails with rock stairs, rock crossings, cathedral trees rising several stories high—oak, ash, poplar. The land is in a trust, the Delaware & Raritan Greenway Land Trust, which means that it can never be developed, and that strangers can hike the well-made trails. Our forest abuts other privately owned and preserved forests and also a stretch belonging to the State of New Jersey. There are neighbors. There is mail and package delivery, the mailbox at the bottom of a long gravel driveway, but somehow the idea of affixing an "address" to this place seems particularly misplaced. The house, near the village of Ringoes—just seventy miles from New York City, fifty miles from Philadelphia, ten miles from Princeton, five miles from Lambertville in the too easily maligned, benighted State of New Jersey—is located in the most densely populated state in the country. Even so, the only thing that arrives from that wider, crowded world is the wind falling into the trees.

In the 1920s, the Farm, as we call it for short, though it is not really a farm at all and never has been in the traditional sense, was a hunting compound of three cottages—two smaller ones and the main house, added onto over the years until, when my stepfather, Dan Sullivan, bought the place in 1970, it looked more like a ranch-style house than a hunting lodge. He bought it from a woman who had recently lost her husband. She had two young sons. She told Dan she couldn't care for the place the way it needed to be cared for without her husband. She told Dan the place needed to be loved.

There were nine children in the house, plus the baby my stepfather and mother had together—so as our blended family came together, lofts rose through the ceilings, a wing extended from one end of the house, transforming a garage into bedrooms. A dining room got pushed out from the kitchen, the walls replaced by plate-glass windows and sliding glass doors so that sitting down for a meal felt like you were hanging above the yard in the trees.

At the far end of the new wing, Dan added an indoor swimming pool that he kept heated at 105 degrees with a furnace all its own. Sliding Japanese doors with their smoked panes sealed in a steam so thick you couldn't see your hand. Dan practiced as a Gestalt therapist, though he wasn't legally licensed, and often, naked, he'd see his patients, also naked, in the pool.

The house itself—wood paneled, stone fireplaces, big, exposed beams—was covered in Haitian art, which Dan, in an antinomian moment of inspiration, collected and hoped to sell. His fascination with Haiti led him somehow to both divorce his wife and then marry my mother there—at least this was what I gleaned as a kid. Whatever the case, for a long while his marriage to my mother wasn't recognized in the state of New Jersey. With each trip, Dan brought back more Haitian art. He bought wood-panel carvings, metal carvings, ebony sculptures, colorful and fantastically naïve images, somber styles, virgins feeding their baby Christs, Eve tempting Adam with forbidden fruit, funeral processions, voodoo ceremonies, an enormous pink fish with a belly filled with a crab eating mangoes. He would unload these marvels on weekend New York sophisticates in his Jacmel Gallery, in New Hope, Pennsylvania, across the Delaware from Lambertville. There was a logic to it all, but over time these works took up residence on our walls, and, like a town committed to an idea—The Home of the World's Largest Corn Palace—the house became a repository for a trend still awaiting its moment.

The place was stuffed with stuff. Dan's first wife, Sally, was a newspaper heiress. Her father had owned the *Times of Trenton* and oil interests in Texas. She inherited eighteenth-century cupboards and cabinets, side tables, Louis Comfort Tiffany objets, Vuitton steamer trunks, a pair of swords that dated to the French Revolution, sterling silver, cranberry crystal, Rosenthal china, Bohemian glass. The house was a kaleidoscopic mix of African and Haitian art, and traditional furniture, dinnerware, and specialized silver dinner implements and doodads—grape shears, a potato fork, a cake breaker, a butter pick—that had no practical contemporary exigence. Plants and books were everywhere. A swinging couch. Persian rugs. An orange laminate kitchen straight out of an electric Kool-Aid acid test. In photographs of the time, usually for holidays and other occasions, Dan could be seen sporting an ascot, jaunty suspenders. On his ring finger sat an enormous turquoise ring. He was a would-be philosopher and a dandy trapped in the body of a Texas showman who loved opera and enjoyed showboating and wrong-footing dinner guests and disarming the locals with a glad hand and a wink.

He and Sally had lived in Africa, London, and Paris, so the house felt like a wing of the British Museum, with all the associated colonialist baggage, in miniature: there were marble busts, African masks and spears, sculptures of Joan of Arc, a bit of ivory and a couple stuffed birds, a puffin. Photographs lined the halls. Along with the portraits taken of us by my mother, there were also portraits of ancestors staring out from another century, forgotten faces squinting back at you from a great distance. There was even a signed portrait of Queen Victoria, hanging there on the wall like a relative. If there was anything for a kid to learn by studying the contents of the house, it seemed to be that history was completely mad, off its rocker, and that history's citizens, at least as pictured here, were pretty grumpy about what had happened.

If you believed this Texas storyteller, who drove into our lives in a turquoise Cadillac belonging to his father-in-law, the whole place was history. According to Dan, the house sat on the site of a sacred Lenape burial ground. He told us that if we looked hard enough, we could find Lenape coins and arrowheads. He told us that George Washington had camped at the foot of our driveway near the Alexauken Creek on his way to defeat the British troops at what is now known as Washington Crossing.

He told us a lot of things when we were kids. John Ringo, founder of our town, had buried a bunch of gold up here. In the evenings sometimes, Dan would have all us kids climb a ladder so we could sit on the roof of one of the barns. He'd light a joint, which he liked to do, and take a deep long puff, then pass it around. From up there, he told us, you could see New York City. This was as untrue then as it is now. You can look as hard as you want from that roof, but you will never see New York City. But that was Dan—and all of us kids looked hard just the same: for the arrowheads, for the Indian coins, for the hidden chest of John Ringo's gold, for New York City. Dan infused everything with a certain kind of magic and lore. The name Omega Farm, for instance, was a nod to his favorite philosopher, Pierre Teilhard de Chardin, who wrote about a future time when everything in the universe spirals into one unified point—the Omega Point. So, Omega Farm—with its tone of utopian aspiration tempered by the common straw of everyday life—suggested the old joke about utopias: that the only thing wrong with them was that they included other people.

BEFORE WE MOVED TO the Farm, my mother, sisters, and I lived just down the road on the outskirts of Princeton in a big white colonial in the woods on Drake's Corner Road. Long after we left Drake's Corner Road for the Farm, I would still consider it my real house, the Farm some kind of fake house, imposter house, temporary house, my real home waiting for me to return to it. In it were my bedroom and my dolls and my things and my family, all ordered and tidy, and built by my mother and father early in their marriage. My parents split up in the spring of 1969, and as I remember it, my mother went to her bed and stayed there for what seemed a long time.

At the suggestion of a friend, my mother started seeing Dan, who ran a Gestalt therapy clinic in Princeton. At the time, he lived there, too, with Sally and their children. In town, Dan had a reputation as a feminist, a supporter of women, even organized sit-ins in pubs that excluded women. Although he was unlicensed, he advertised himself as a therapist and worked with groups on realizing sexual equality. His thesis was essentially sound: the dehumanizing role we ascribe to women was good for neither sex. Only if men and women could be equal could true romantic love be achieved. But he was also something of a con man, a serial philanderer. He was, as people sometimes like to say, a complicated figure, a charismatic figure, a man who was convinced he was helping women realize their full potential. If he sometimes slept with those same women—well, it was the seventies, after all. For Christmas one year, he gave me a punching bag to toughen me up; another year, for the same reason, he gave me a BB gun. I absorbed the rightness of his cause, on my behalf, and on the behalf of all women, and us kids threw ourselves into the project with the full conviction and certainty of a just cause. He gave all of us stickers that read THIS AD INSULTS WOMEN, THIS MOVIE INSULTS WOMEN, THIS BOOK INSULTS WOMEN, and he encouraged us to stick them everywhere that warranted them. And we did, marching all over Princeton, into stores and movie theaters, slapping those stickers onto everything that offended us—but that was later.

As it happened, Dan's clinic was located in a dilapidated farmhouse just a short distance through the woods from our house. Mom got herself out of her bed and made her way to one of those sessions and soon she fell in love.

BY THE SUMMER OF 1970, his kids and the four of us were traveling out west together, crammed into the back of a camper that was perched on the back of a pickup truck. We drove all over California and Oregon, stayed with friends of Dan's who "hated" children, distant relatives who hardly recalled how we were related—the nine children spilling from the camper to take over the house and lives of whoever was hosting us. In Big Sur, we stayed at the Esalen Institute, where the adults wandered around naked, to the mortification of us kids, while Dan held group therapy sessions.

As children, we were divided into the "big kids" and the "little kids." I was second youngest, a little kid—until Mom and Dan had the baby, Joan. In San Francisco, the big kids got to accompany Mom and Dan to a production of *Hair*, regaling the rest of us with stories of the cast naked on stage. Naked was a theme, a prolonged seventies-era meme. All the way through Oregon, up into Washington and the Cascades, the kids sang "Aquarius" and "Manchester England" and "Frank Mills," dreamy and longing, which made all of us want to find a man named Frank Mills.

The trip ended with three of us—Dan's daughter Carrie, my sister Sarah, and me—lost deep in the Cascade mountains. We were on a five-day hiking trip. I had stopped to rest. Sarah and Carrie stopped with me to be sure I wasn't alone. When we started again, we took a wrong turn. Night came on and it was very dark so we unfurled our sleeping bags at the edge of the trail, each of us taking turns watching for the coyotes we could hear howling in the distance.

Mom and Dan and the other kids stumbled onto a cabin where a bunch of geologists lived. They were eating their dinner and offered our group what remained. Everyone was hungry because we hadn't packed enough food for the trip and had already run low. Mom and Dan told them they'd lost three of their children. The geologists set off to find us, leaving the others to finish the leftovers—which they did, every last bite. Nothing remained, not even a scrap. Eventually, they found us in our spot at the edge of the trail. I was five years old; Carrie was eight; Sarah was nine.

We were now a family of some kind. It didn't matter that Dan was still married to Sally, that we still lived on Drake's Corner Road, that the Sullivans were moving from Princeton to the Farm, and that my parents were in the midst of a bitter divorce that somehow involved the courts declaring that we, the McPhee girls, were not allowed to see Dan Sullivan or Yolanda Harrop—my father's girl-friend. I can still remember the name of my father's lawyer, Princi-pato, called Prince. I had thought his first name was Prince and his last name Appato. My mother would be frequently distraught by the bad deals Principato tried to make for alimony and child support, yelling and crying about the pittance. "Who can live on that?" Mom would shout, her expression a mix of fear and hatred that terrified me as I also calculated my value based on the amount offered for our support. I thought Principato was an evil prince.

My mother's lawyer was Henry Hill, a fat, jolly man who had a desperate crush on my mother. He had a little airplane and he'd fly us places for the day—to Maine, to go to the beach, to dig for clams. Some days he'd simply fly upside down above our house, later at the Farm. "It's Henry," Mom would say with her smile, pointing at the sky.

No one cared about the law. We saw Yolanda. We saw Dan. He'd come to our house on Drake's Corner Road in the middle of the night and park his Cadillac in the woods. On the way to school, we'd see it from the window of the bus, lurking there in the trees. But we kept quiet.

After Dan and Sally bought the Farm, we would drive out from Princeton for the afternoon and end up spending the night. Though their marriage was coming apart, still sometimes Sally was there, which was just plain awkward, though Sally never made me feel it; she was kind and gentle and always interested in anything us kids had to say.

On one early occasion visiting the Farm, we brought our new puppy, a sheepdog with long curly white hair. He had a name, Maximilian de Winter, that seemed to call for an ascot, and we loved him. He drowned in the indoor swimming pool, found by my sister Sarah, whose scream I can still hear. Another beloved dog of ours, Smokey, came with us for a visit and was run over, one of her hind legs crushed beyond repair.

THE BEAUTY OF THE natural world wasn't something I was able to appreciate as a kid. The Farm was in the woods, but I was no Emerson or Thoreau. There were so many kids. The two cottages were filled with teenagers, friends of Danny and Mary, Dan's two oldest—kids with names like Dougal and Janice and Snooky, Pat, Marvin, and Martin. They were both Black and white. They listened to Janice Joplin and Jimi Hendrix, smoked and drank. The vast field in front of the house and abutting our lawn belonged to a man named Heston, which made me think of Charlton Heston, and in summertime this field was always tall with corn. In that corn, the big kids, and Dan, grew pot, and Dan always worried that any helicopter flying overhead was the police. His worry made us all fearful. On a couple occasions the police actually did come, one time in spectacular cinematic fashion (so recorded in family lore), descending on ropes from a helicopter to find and confiscate the pot in the field, pulling it from the ground, then flying off again. I do not actually believe this happened, but there was a penchant for dramatic stories and they had a way of becoming part of the family narrative. Ditch weed is what the Big Kids called Dan's pot.

If we were financially comfortable, the McPhee family, the Sullivans were rich. Their mother took them on exotic trips—to Martinique, to Hawaii. They had a beloved nanny who had worked for them for years. Her name was Bertha and she lived in Trenton but was too old to care for them. She cooked a favorite cake of theirs that Dan would drive to Trenton to pick up from her, bringing it home to his kids, who savored it like gold. They had a bulldog named Peggy and a golden retriever named OJ for O. J. Simpson. Everything was OJ—clothes, sheets, towels, helmets. On the vast front lawn, they played endless games of football, which my sisters and I eventually did, too, the towering ash trees marking the end zones, Dan drawing plays on his palm. There was an immediate hierarchy: Sullivans on the top; McPhees on the bottom. My sisters and I listened to Dan; Dan's kids did not listen to Mom—or so it seemed to me.

At night, the dinner table was crowded and often argumentative, the tectonic pressures, resentments, shifting allegiances, and betrayals of two very different families suddenly erupting, say, over the issue of abortion. *Roe v. Wade* was very much in the news. As a Catholic, Dan was stridently against abortion, even though swirling among the children whispers passed from ear to ear, could be true or not true, that my mother had been pregnant twice before giving birth to Joan. I didn't understand exactly what this meant as a child, but I absorbed it enough to know my mother was going through something big and scary that she was trying to fix. When she went away one weekend (to have an abortion, I imagined then, believe now), my sisters and I stayed with our father, who by 1972 was living with Yolanda and her four children at her house in Princeton. It wasn't Dad's weekend, so it felt like we got something extra, but getting something also furthered my perception that all was not right, and rather that something was very wrong. I wrote my mother a letter. All it said was "I love you." I wrote the words many times across the front and the back of the page. Then I folded it, stole a stamp from my father's desk in his office at Yolanda's house. I dropped the letter in the mailbox just outside her front door and raised the red flag. My father and Yolanda discovered the letter, read it, and were alarmed, worried, I suppose, about the burden of my attachment to Mom—or perhaps my desperate need to reassure her with my love. She was only gone for the weekend, and they had no idea (I don't believe) about the abortion, that she was suffering. They told me, sitting with me in Dad's office, that Mom knew that I loved her.

* * *

DAN AND THE BIG kids would fight about abortion using terms I didn't understand, words like *quickening* and *sentient* flying across the table, the tide of rage rising. When it wasn't abortion, it was the PLO, the Palestine Liberation Organization, and Israel. Always the same fights, which went so late into the night that Mom would disappear into Dan's bedroom, lulled to sleep by the rhythms of Dan's mildly subversive waterbed, a word that, by itself, conjures an entire gaudy family, long extinct, of 1970s-era enthusiasms that populated the house—fondue pots, egg-shaped cocoon chairs suspended from the high branches of an oak, swinging in the air—while my sisters and I found a place to sleep on the floor in the living room, curling into each other, wondering how we'd get to school in the morning.

IN THE FALL OF 1969, my parents only recently separated, Mom still in her bed, my father's roommate from college, Bo Goldman; his wife, Mab; and several of their many children moved in with my sisters, Mom, and me at Drake's Corner Road. They were very poor. Bo was a struggling screenwriter and wasn't having any luck selling his scripts to Hollywood. Mab made stuffed animals for children, sewed them herself, to bring in some extra cash. Mom was struggling and neither family could make ends meet, so the idea was that together we'd have more, and life would be easier. My mother was always very busy wanting to help other people. It was as if by helping others she was helping herself, by fixing others she was fixing herself, but it never quite seemed to work out that way. Bo moved into Dad's office in the garage and worked there. Mab took over the house, the kitchen, and started feeding us organic foods—things like Tiger's Milk and liver, lots of beans. Their kids moved into our bedrooms, sharing them with us. Mab became the gatekeeper of our world and Mom surrendered to her. Mom liked to do that, too, cede control, let others decide for her. Mab made it her job to keep my father out. He left; he had no business returning. When he picked us up for school, she would not allow him to drive up to the house, physically blocking his car by standing at the foot of the driveway. At one point she erected a chain between two trees so that his car could not pass. She changed our telephone number and would not let my sisters and me know the new number. If we learned the number—my sister Sarah would go sleuthing until she found it—Mab changed it again. She didn't want our father to know it. There was no reason for this other than to punish Dad.

The Goldmans stayed with us for a couple of years and then moved to Hollywood. In the late 1970s Bo became famous for the script to *One Flew Over the Cuckoo's Nest*, followed by *Melvin and Howard*, for which he received his second Oscar, followed by *Shoot the Moon*—the story of my parents' divorce, likely written while he lived with us, typing away in my father's office in the garage.

THE BACK AND FORTH between Princeton and Ringoes, between my old home and what was becoming my new home, ended in the spring of 1973. My parents were finally divorced, and my mother was very pregnant with Joan. Was this to be the Omega Point? The only point that Omega Farm represented to me then was the upheaval and disorder of a momentary whim that had gone off the rails. In the mornings, we were always late to school, piled into the Cadillac. Many times, I went to school wearing two different shoes. Afternoons, one of the friends of my older stepbrother, long hair flying, a cigarette in one hand, a beer between his legs, would pull into the school parking lot like an extra from *Easy Rider,* rev the car engine so that everyone in the straitlaced, buttoned-down world of Princeton could watch me climb into the back of the Turquoise Cadillac and thereby become properly, righteously, discomfited.

WE ATE DINNER VERY late, my mother, now a photographer, returning from work with the camera bags hanging off her shoulders, my stepfather sometimes glowering with rage. The abortion and PLO arguments that could swell to violence were well underway. All his life, Dan held forth, center stage, leveraging his Texas drawl when it suited his audience, and never once did he seem to decline a pleasing impulse. He had studied to be a Jesuit priest at Grand Coteau in Louisiana but had been expelled for having sex with another novitiate. He had affairs easily. He smoked too much pot, drank too much wine, took LSD with RD Laing on several occasions—just to see what it was like. As a child, I had no idea who RD Laing was, but just the way the story was told, the way the name was said, added to the mythos of Dan. Dan and Mom were always rushing off to the car, ice clinking in drinks in hand, late to the symphony or the opera in Philadelphia or New York.

I thought it best to stay quiet and not draw attention to myself, but I watched and here is what I saw: adults stoned or drunk or exhausted or all three; children filled with turbulence and rage—pushed together and told to get along—stealing each other's clothes and small possessions; children who played mean tricks on each other, laughed, forgave each other, went on adventures, prattled in the wee hours about nothing, but mostly—and this was because of the older kids, who could sniff out a fraud when they saw it—mocked and ironized to a fare-thee-well the way Omega Farm was neither one thing nor the other, neither farm nor utopia, but mostly, really, a big sprawling, chaotic mess with Neil Young playing from speakers nailed to the trees.

DAN WAS A HANDSOME man, thinning hair, blue eyes. He wore a cowboy hat and had a half squint that, when focused on you, could make you feel like the most special person in the world. He played poker with wealthy men in town, town being Princeton, and with some of the police. When he won, he shared the wealth, handing out bills to us, and he won a lot. He wore his ascots and his cravats and his brightly colored pants half-ironically. He loved people, an audience. The house was always filled. There were frequent parties—the lawn taken over by champagne and hot-air balloons lifting into the evening sky. We were always in debt, the taxman was always coming for us—but no matter, it didn't interfere with Dan's vision. An orchard, a hedge of forsythia against the field to serve as a snow fence a quarter mile long, sunshine yellow in the spring, a garden overflowing with vegetables and flowers in summer. We raised sheep, goats, a donkey, peacocks, ducks. We ate the lamb for Christmas and Easter. The chickens laid eggs that we collected in the morning and at dusk, finding them in their nest boxes like a surprise each time. A local farmer harvested grass for feed from our field. For a few years, we even had a raspberry farm.

AND THEN WE ALL grew up and moved away, the ten of us spreading across the country, many of us vowing never to return. "The scene of the crime of my childhood," one of my sisters said. My stepfather died in 1994 of pancreatic cancer. We married, had children, developed our careers, grew older ourselves. My mother started forgetting things, slowly yet steadily—one by one our names slipping away along with all else.

But something happened.

Sitting on the deck above the lawn at dusk, my kids, their cousins, would sometimes declare their own love, too, for the majesty of the view as the sun slid west, its colors leaking across a horizon punctuated in the distance by a hot-air balloon. It brought to mind all the many sunsets that came before—the garden parties and pig roasts, the football games, the tobogganing down the hill, the weddings, the quiet evenings with my mother sipping a glass of wine. The slow, majestic beauty of an afternoon as it built toward sunset was something I'd enjoyed but never treasured, at least not until the kids, these teenagers growing into adults, who had no deep past here, but now understanding what was what, had said it. What they were saying indirectly, I realized, was that it would be a shame if we lost this view, if we lost the Farm.

This was suddenly, bracingly, a likelihood. My mother, who had somehow kept everything afloat, was slipping away. Who would oversee taking care of her? How would we afford it, and where? The first question would be answered by default. My sisters had done well, had made their own lives, had their own homes Elsewhere. I lived closest to the Farm and still held on with an inexplicable grip. The second question, *the how*, emerged as a plan in which my sisters and I contributed money to an account managed by my sister Sarah in Atlanta, which she used to pay the caregiver. Mom had not saved for retirement and had no money beyond the value of her house. Everyone knew the answer to the *where* question: the research on "aging in place" had made it clear. People liked to grow old where they had lived their lives, at home, where things were familiar. The Farm was an extant, practical solution to the quandary of caring for our mother in a place where she would be happiest and in a manner my sisters and I could, conceivably, afford. A nursing home was none of these things. We would keep my mother at the Farm for as long as we could.

At the grim peak of the pandemic, the dark December month of a year in which nearly six thousand long-term elderly residents of nursing homes were, each week, dying in unspeakable conditions, alone, afraid, cut off from anything or anyone they had ever known, I walked out into the night, the ground covered in snow, the wind whistling through the branches of the oak trees, and thanked each lucky star above my head.

History, like the wind clicking in the frozen branches of the oaks, would likely view such moments with a cold objective eye. This, too, history might say, in echo of a phrase I was hearing increasingly, is what white privilege looks like—that Dan, a New Age, would-be guru, had once purchased a farm, way back when. That I—if I or anyone cared to listen to what was written in the wind—was heir to a first and second national crime: first, to lands that had been systematically stolen from the Lenape and the tribes of the First People; and second, to land and property—those ever-powerful Lockean points of economic leverage—that had been systematically withheld from emancipated slaves and their descendants. The world made from these two great errors was in flames. The smoke from forest fires in California made smog in the skies over New York City. Other great American cities were being torn apart by state-sanctioned police violence against people protesting police violence against people of color. Meanwhile, the pandemic: the onrush, the overwhelming flow of bodies stacking up in outdoor refrigerated trailers in parking lots of besieged hospitals because we couldn't bury or burn them fast enough. It was a grotesque cascading state of failure made worse by a punishing and incompetent regime of elected officials who seemed to follow some hidden hand that moved all things, all important decisions, toward choices and public proclamations that defied common sense, that a fifth grader would know were genuinely insane.

It will be for others to unravel the great chain of causation, to name the actors, and in some way to remember, to their everlasting shame, the scoundrels of this history, against which each of us responded, as we could, in whatever context and circumstance we found ourselves. Mine, for a brief moment, was to recognize one single life, my mother's, who had given life to me, to bear witness as she slowly came unmoored, and, as my mother became a ghost, to find a way to hold on to that remnant of her, the Farm, that I might find—and further—its purpose.

BEFORE THE PANDEMIC, I didn't think in those terms. My thoughts, such as they were, were naïve. On weekend visits, I began taking on some project or other that needed attention, usually the ones that added to the experience of being there—and to the ones that didn't, I failed to notice or turned a blind eye. I liked to think of myself as clever and resourceful.

At the edge of the forest, surrounded by thickets and brambles, trees dripping with vines, we had an old Sylvan pool, kidney shaped and very large at forty thousand gallons. An old, partially collapsed tarp revealed a swampy green murk with frogs and floaters and snakes. There was never enough money to do things right. A tarp was not a pool cover. The pool deck was brick, but the bricks were in disrepair—pushed upward or sunken by the rising or sinking roots of nearby trees. I decided one year, not long before the pandemic, that I'd re-lay the bricks, push back the brambles, and create a path down from the house. My mother loved to swim. The path to the pool was paved in small sharp stones that hurt her feet. I also decided I'd buy a proper pool cover. I paid for all this by selling discarded things from the house at the local flea market, old knick-knacks of my grandmother's.

In the basement Mom had forty years of negatives from her job as a photographer in Princeton. Visiting one weekend, I answered the phone. It was an old customer asking if, by chance, Mom had retained the negatives of his wedding, and if so, could he buy them? This question led me to the loft of the barn adjacent to the house, where hundreds of thousands of negatives lay stored by year and alphabet. One Thanksgiving, with Sarah, my children, and their cousins, we formed a human chain, and box by box moved all the negatives to the basement, where I organized them. I started with the most recent work, and when I could I made calls—cold calls— to Mom's former customers and asked if they wanted to buy their negatives. Many of them did. Little by little, the pool became a place where people wanted to swim. Swimming was the one remaining area of independence for my mother. I loved swimming with her or sitting poolside and watching her execute a perfect, YMCA-trained sidestroke up and down the length of the pool. I loved that her work paid for the repairs.

Unable to afford an actual house, I used my mother's house to play house, at scale. I wanted it always to be a place for family and friends and people wandering up the driveway to come together. Fixing Mom's house became a way of preserving and possibly even correcting the past, creating a place where the kids could visit their grandmother, a place where, we later joked, my husband and I, and our friends, and all the siblings, could retire and putter around in the garden, a utopian retirement community of old fogies writing stories and playing music—that vision, even as a joke, held sway.

"Don't be so romantic," my oldest sister, Laura, said to me many times. "That place will eat you alive."

Twice I had tried to buy the Farm (as beautiful as it is, it isn't worth very much), but twice my sisters, for practical reasons, weren't ready to have Mom sell it. Even so, I would never, not ever, have moved to the Farm.

T hen history happened, as we all know so well.

In March of 2020, against the entanglements of the pandemic, against the better judgment of my sisters, I returned to my childhood home from New York City with two teenage children, my husband, and our cat and dog so we could shelter in place with my ailing mother. My sisters were scattered and weren't in a position to do this, and someone needed to relieve Dayana, the caregiver. My son was a sophomore in high school, my daughter, Livia, a sophomore in college. My husband and I are writers and professors. We moved in, set up desks, learned to Zoom, and tried to make something of it.

I found myself working in the room my maternal grandmother had occupied at the end of her life, which had remained essentially unchanged since she'd left it twenty-five years earlier, with photographs of her family, my ancestors, watching me from the walls. I was on the verge of publishing a novel based on her life, tracing its path from Ohio to Montana to New Jersey across the twentieth century. When I gave Zoom readings, people liked seeing the old photographs in the background. Grammy's feathered hats, her beaver coat, and her opera capes still hung in the closet, as if waiting for her to return. Sometimes, late into the night, I'd sit on a chaise on a little deck on the other side of a sliding glass door, just outside the bedroom, listen to the tree frogs, and think about how I'd make the best of this situation.

In the beginning, my ambitions were quaint—I planted a garden in the Garden State, made some landscaping improvements, moving peonies from shade to sunshine, that sort of thing. Along with many thousands of other people, I went out to buy baby chicks. I didn't want just any chicks. I wanted chicks that would lay colorful eggs, exotic chicks—Araucanas, Marans, Sapphire Olive Eggers, California White, Black Australorps. We set up a big dog crate in the kitchen and created a miniature farm with warming lights, and we raised the chicks there for the next two months, my mother spending hours watching and holding them, the kitchen filling with a thin layer of dust.

I rallied the family, and we turned over the dirt in the deserted garden, created beds, and by the end of March we had more than a hundred onion sets planted, along with beets, spinach, kale, and lettuce. I had never planted a garden before. It was a warm spring, the days like May. In the Before Times, on our way from New York for a weekend, Jasper would sometimes ask what each of us would bring to the Farm "for the zombie apocalypse." It was a recurring debate, and his answer would vary depending on what new piece of technology he'd been reading about: "Drones," he'd say. "Medical supplies and antibiotics," Livia might say. "A Phalanx CIWS, Close-in Weapon System," my husband might say—a rapid-fire, computer-controlled radar-guided gun that can fire forty-five hundred rounds per minute, knock missiles out of the sky, or zombies, say, hobbling through the fields toward the house. "Seeds," I always said. My answer never varied.

ONE NIGHT WHILE WALKING with the dogs under the moon, we heard a high-pitched, descending cry that sounded like someone being stabbed repeatedly. We googled "fox call sound," and sure enough we heard again the scream that had stopped us in our tracks. Long ago, my stepfather disappeared into the night. My mother had worried. When he finally reappeared, a little drunk, a little high, he told her he'd been out in the fields listening for foxes. In Grammy's room, late in the night, we could hear something that in all the years of growing up on the Farm I never once heard: far down in the swale, where the fields met the woods, the wild, piercing howl of coywolves. The chorus was set at the stratospheric limits of the vocal register, each voice a virtuosic act at two a.m., and it cut right through you. Our dogs charged out of the house to the edge of the lawn facing the forest and made a great barking show of force, my mother's dog, a big black Lab named Leo, booming his low percussive notes, our Italian water dog reaching for the upper register. Then something marvelous and caveman-like happened: the sharp barking racket of our dogs switched over, suddenly, into a sustained, if wavering, melodic line. The wild creatures of the woods had called out to their domesticated cousins, who responded, across a dark divide, joining them in kind, in song. At two a.m., as I was half asleep, it seemed like music for the zombie apocalypse.

* * *

A HANDYMAN WITH A thick Australian accent who called himself Aussie Bob helped me string an electrified fence to keep the foxes out of the chicken coop. We hadn't yet moved it outside, but I was preparing. The chickens needed to be at least six weeks old, and the temperature outside needed to be in the sixties. In the past, we had lost many a chicken to the foxes. We were urban apartment dwellers suddenly without our super but armed with the internet. It was *The Decameron* meets Tractor Supply Company. *Green Acres*, with kids—teenagers who were stuck living with their parents, a husband and wife unaccustomed to a new and unfamiliar daily proximity to each other *all the time. Zombie apocalypse*, only we still had our jobs. There were pay cuts, but our jobs were still there. We were by no means rich or well off, and, in fact, like so many other Americans, we were sliding deeply into debt. We weren't dead, not yet anyway, but collectively, as a family, we would come to drive one another a little crazy. My mother's mind slowly crumbled, and a madness seemed writ large on a horizon that stretched well beyond the Farm. After fixing the coop, Aussie Bob asked me, with his eyes squinting in the sunlight, if I'd stocked up on ammo.

"On what?" I asked.

"Ammunition," he said, holding on to me with his small eyes.

"Why would I need that?" I asked, with genuine bafflement.

"There's a run on it," he said. "They'll be shutting down the fueling stations. Then they'll be coming for your food."

And so, from a place on a hilltop in the benchlands of the Delaware River, surrounded by forest and farms with barns that said "Vote Trump," a place where 4-H is still a thing, where you can still hear the highway but you can also, on moonlit nights when the wind is right, hear the heart-creasing howl of the foxes and coywolves, a place where I and my sisters grew up and, perhaps because of the ghost notes of memory, a place in which none of us ever wanted to make a life, here, I found myself—confronted, as all of us were, with ourselves, with the flags under which we had sailed, and the disquieting prospect of armed citizens approaching to lay siege to our zucchinis.

IN THE MEANTIME, YEARS of deferred maintenance had left me with a multitudinous, variated, and distracting mess to contemplate. I had always known this about the Farm, but I'd been a weekend guest and my eye had been on the pool. It was easy to ignore a lot when you didn't live here, to overlook a problem. But now the problems seemed to call me out. I couldn't leave them behind because I wasn't leaving. Stink bugs and cave crickets, mice and spiders used untrimmed limbs from the oaks that towered above the house as freeways to the kitchen and other rooms, sneaking through cracks to get inside. Any which way they could, they found an entrance in. The forest, too, advanced on the house like a slow-motion army. I could watch this, almost, from my desk in Grammy's room.

In those early days, it occurred to me to maybe fix up a few things in the yard and around the house, actual problems. Little things at first, like the flower bed outside my window, which was overgrown and encroaching on the house. I weeded it, mulched it, planted a white lilac. There was a dead tree in the yard, an ash, one of many trees towering above our little world. But this ash was dead, and it bothered my mother. She would point to it and indicate that it needed to go. Even though it rose a story or two, it could easily come down with a chainsaw and know-how. I hired a guy who climbed the tree to bring down the crown, branch by branch. After that he cut a wedge in the base of the trunk and then tied a chain around the tree, hooked the chain to his pickup, and pulled the rest of the tree down by driving fast across the yard. He cut up the trunk and we split it into firewood, rented a stump grinder, raked the splash, and had a bonfire. The tree that had marked the endzone in our childhood football games, huddled with Dan drawing plays on his palm with his finger, was no more.

I called the exterminator. I called the plumber to fix the kitchen drain, which had long ago been diverted in some handyman's hurried (or, more likely, stoned) mind so that it spilled soapy dishwasher water into the front yard from a long and yellowed PVC pipe. Every time we ran the dishwasher, suds poured into the emerging daylilies.

Mom and Dan, in keeping with the quasi-communal spirit of the place, had always welcomed people here. It seemed anyone could join the sprawling, mixed family of kids, friends, and assorted strangers who might wander up the gravel driveway for a visit and then, because my stepfather had discovered in them something useful or interesting (they could repair things, say, like kitchen drains), they might stay on, sometimes for years. The ex-boyfriend of a sister's childhood friend came to a party and left ten years later. He lived in the indoor swimming pool, by then defunct. It had been poorly constructed, and the steam ate through the walls and threatened to topple it. His name was Sergey, known as Serge. He shored up the walls, put some planks across the hole where the pool had been, made a loft in the rafters upon which he put a mattress, and called it good. There was no bathroom, no heat, no insulation, but somehow he lived there for a long time, doing odd jobs for Dan—handyman jobs—one of which included building a barn. This former stranger was Russian and knew about barns. He built a new barn, designing a second story that became an office for Dan. The bottom of the barn had three bays, each one a receptacle for junk—screens and doors and glass of all sorts, tarps and old furniture, shoved in there in case they could be useful later on. No one, it seemed, ever threw anything away.

ANOTHER STRANGER WAS A different sister's boyfriend's best friend from college. They'd grown up together, gone to college together, been athletic stars. This friend of the boyfriend came for a weekend, and he, too, stayed for many years. He was a preppy sort, wore Lacoste and chinos, penny loafers with pennies in the hold. He had jobs in New York, a fancy car, big ambitions for what he could achieve on Wall Street, but somehow his residence was at the Farm. I'm not sure what he contributed, but he stayed long after my sister and the boyfriend had broken up. He stayed and stayed and stayed, until my sister, now married, said to my mother that she had to make a choice: me or Him. My mother chose Him. And for a few years my sister refused to visit.

EARLIER, MANY YEARS EARLIER, soon after her divorce, my mother plunged, headlong, with her friend Elaine, into running a local photography studio in Princeton. They bought the business from Ulli Steltzer, a German photographer who was well-known around the country for her work photographing families and famous locals from Princeton. She was moving to Canada. For $3,000 Mom and Elaine bought the studio on Tulane Street and set up shop.

They were two mid-century women, Pryde and Elaine, raised, educated, groomed to be attractive, supportive homemakers for their men. My mother had gone to Sweet Briar College in Virginia. It was expected that you graduated with an engagement ring. She could write poetry, read poetry, dress impeccably while discussing literature and philosophy. She was properly finished at finishing school.

But the times, they were a-changing. Men vanished. New men entered the scene. Pryde's new man, Dan, finally divorced Sally legally and was granted alimony and child support by the courts of New Jersey, a first in the state for a man. While he worked on his group therapy visions, took care of stuff around the house, wrote some articles, Mom honed her business skills. Soon, Elaine sold her share, and, with a new shingle, now on Chambers Street, in downtown Princeton—Pryde Brown Photographs—my mother began working full-time, every day and almost every weekend, and would continue to do so, perpetually on the go, for the next forty years.

For all those years, people at the Farm came and went, wandered about, used the toilets and broke things. As a result, there was a jerry-rigged, ad hoc, suspended-by-a-thread quality to everything one touched.

A lot needed fixing.

The phone would ring. Something was broken. You'd scratch at a problem—a little blemish, a busted valve or missing pipe, an unpleasant odor coming from somewhere behind one of the outbuildings.

If I hadn't noticed these problems on weekend visits . . . or if I'd allowed them to recede from my mind the moment I left . . . now I couldn't *unsee* them. There was junk absolutely everywhere. Fifty years of junk had found hiding places in the various barns, in the indoor pool, in the trees. Railroad ties, shingles, an entire deck that had once spanned the length of the house had been dumped in the forest behind the pool. Old trampolines, old swing sets, so much glass—it was everywhere. Tires, an oil tank, scraps of metal, mattresses, box springs. I thought of the movie *Sex, Lies, and Videotape*. One of the characters contemplates all the garbage of the world, becomes anxious about the fate of everyone's garbage. Our garbage, tossed in the woods as if the woods would simply eat it up, made me not only anxious (how in the world will we get rid of all this—"Dig a hole," one of my sisters said) but upset, mad even. I'd stand over a large ball of electrical wire the size of a doghouse and wonder about that moment, long ago, when someone decided it was easier to toss a ball of wire into the woods than to properly dispose of it. Multiply that moment by many decades of similar decision-making and soon you need a dumpster or two, or ten.

You did what you could. Into dumpsters went the garbage: the old sinks, the tires, the swing sets, the tattered blue tarps, the rusted Schwinn bicycles, and the deer bones. After three dumpsters, we hadn't made a dent. The dumpsters cost money that my husband and I paid. My mother didn't have any extra money. I considered it a form of rent—but really it was some kind of neurosis. I would leave the place a little better than I found it. I'd be good. I'd do right. I'd fix. I'd solve. I'd make better. I'd restore, repair, mend. But if Mom didn't have any extra money, neither did we. What was I doing this for? I'd often ask myself. Was I just falling back into old familiar patterns?

FOR AS LONG AS I could remember we'd been working to "save" the Farm. The taxman was always walking up the driveway, or at least that was the way it seemed. I'd even look sometimes to see if I could see him. The wolf was at the door. We knew that Dan awaited alimony payments, child support payments that would solve things, but local businesses would always be calling about late payments. "The check is in the mail," we were told to say.

On weekends we had workdays, the ten of us kids working eight-hour days filling potholes in the driveway, moving furniture around, fixing the endless problems, dumping junk in the woods—all of us always coming up with excuses to get out of working. If a workday fell on your birthday, you didn't have to work. You got the day off, could sit around watching the others work. It felt good, like you'd gotten something for nothing. We were always trying to get something for nothing. We tried coming up with our own lists of what needed to be done. Once I decided I needed to make croissants, thought Dan would appreciate them because he had a soft spot for food and liked to encourage our interests and hobbies. Cooking was mine. I got pretty far along with the croissants, rolling out the cold butter, folding it, rolling the pastry some more. Dan asked what I was doing. I explained. "That's not a job, Babe." Other kids hid, others pretended they were working; others made excuses so they could be far away from home.

Meanwhile, Mom went off to work and Dan came up with schemes to raise money—compromises and creative solutions to make it all work. There was always an urgency to this. In order to get stuff done that us kids couldn't do on a workday, build a barn for instance, more compromises were made. People who wandered up the driveway, who came for a weekend and never left, were taken in and put to work. Mom used her talents as a photographer to barter; Dan traded therapy for chimney repair. It was catch as catch can, with all these people we bartered with having their own sets of rationalizations and justifications for whatever it was that they were skimming off the top. Indeed, everyone was trying to get something for nothing, or at least for a little bit less. When the dining room was being built, stuff went missing—small things at first, a silver bowl, a marble bust, then bigger things: a Persian rug, a side table, a chair, a Haitian painting. One day Dan paid the carpenter a visit at his home. In plain sight was all our stuff.

One year the oil heater broke down and we couldn't afford to replace it. This lasted a few years. Through several bitter winters with the blizzards of the kind we had back then, we had no heat. There was no deal that could be forged with the company that replaced furnaces. Dan bought a few kerosene heaters and placed them strategically around the house, and this was how we stayed warm.

(A friend recently asked how we kept the pool heated, if we kept the pool heated, when the furnace in the house was broken. The indoor pool had its own furnace, and that furnace wasn't broken.)

Christmas rolled around. Dan's mother, Merle, would arrive from Dallas, a tall woman with a crown of snow-white hair and a thick Texas drawl. She'd bring many presents, impeccably wrapped, from Neiman Marcus. Born in 1900, she was the age of the year, a phrase she liked to repeat. We'd buy an enormous tree, trim it with popcorn and cranberries we'd string ourselves, with white lights and ornaments carefully preserved in cushioned boxes in the basement. Pulling the ornaments from their boxes was a surprise each time, cloisonné bulbs, smoked glass bulbs, intricately painted bulbs.

Dan would give us $75 apiece to use for buying Christmas presents for each other—ten kids, two parents. I always wanted to keep the money for myself. On Christmas Eve we'd have a feast, eating one of our lambs. We'd sing carols, read *The Night Before Christmas*, listen to St. Nicholas lumber across the roof as he shouted, "Ho, ho, ho." The big kids encouraged the little kids to believe even though we no longer did.

In the morning presents spilled from beneath the tree deep into the living room. Presents everywhere. Electric toys churned away, alive, doing their thing—little skiers marching up ski lifts to ski down ski slopes, trains going round and round elaborate tracks. We woke up to this, ten stuffed stockings hanging all around the enormous mouth of the fireplace.

When my maternal grandmother visited for the holidays from her house in Maine, she often argued with my mother. Grammy hated the Farm, had a low opinion of Dan, would say to Mom, "You've let yourself go." They'd scream at each other, the fight ending with Grammy, bundled in her black sealskin coat, dragging her suitcases down the long driveway, threatening to hitchhike home. She called the Farm a "den of iniquity."

Cold Decembers, Dan would get a notion and all of us would pack into the van we had, and we'd drive down to Key West, Florida, stay at the Pier House Hotel on the water, watch the sunset and eat Key lime pie and conchs, the taxman and the furnace a distant memory, far away in New Jersey.

* * *

IN THESE YEARS, IN the summers we traveled. We went to Haiti and Mexico, took the Cadillac and a Jeep we had and explored the west, sleeping in cornfields, hiking in canyons—Bryce, Zion, the Grand Canyon, roaming the landscape of John Wayne westerns, which Dan's kids watched endlessly on the *CBS Late Movie*. We traveled— the financial problems kept at bay by ignoring them and racking up debt that someone else somewhere would pay for somehow. Dan and Mom liked to say that travel was the most important form of education. They didn't care if we missed school. In fact, Dan's kids hardly went to school. In the early days, they went to a school called Erehwon, "nowhere" spelled backward—part of the free school movement of the era, schools born of the counterculture and that challenged traditional education. I was jealous because all day they were allowed to choose what they wanted to do and mostly they chose to play. I hated school and stopped going regularly myself in the fourth and fifth grade, until I missed so much the principal got involved and then my father.

When we traveled, nothing seemed to matter about our lives back in New Jersey. In Haiti, we rented a house in the Creole town of Jacmel, a French house with a latticed balcony overlooking the sea, with high ceilings and ceiling fans that whirred across the hot hot days. We had gone there with Dan's business partner, Cathy; Mom; and all of us kids. The idea was to buy Haitian art for the gallery he had opened in New Hope. Cathy and Dan were close, maybe even lovers. A sense I had, like Mom's abortions, that just floated around in the air for us to absorb peripherally and not completely or fully understand. We were kids. I was a kid, trying to interpret the adult world, what they did, how they behaved, what was right, what was wrong. The idea of a lover or an affair with another woman stimulated the imagination—made me want to know more, even if "more" was always opaque and channeled through my child's mind, and plenty of innuendo. When my kids were little, Mark and I said they had elephant ears; they could hear and understand everything even if we thought we hadn't spoken a word.

In Pétion-Ville in the hills above Port-au-Prince, a fancy neighborhood, we went to a party hosted by a gallerist and filled with suave-looking artists who came to speak with Dan, well-dressed men, all men. I remember most the contrast to the rest of the poverty-stricken country, the house and the food and the wine, the air fragrant with tropical flowers—we could have been in Beverly Hills.

In Jacmel, I saw a hungry woman die on the street just outside the market where flies crawled all over the fish and meat, merchants carrying enormous baskets on their heads, police standing guard on the street corners, machine guns slung over their shoulders, Jean-Claude Duvalier, Baby Doc, son of Papa Doc, ruling with his terrifying name—names that seared the imagination. Dan told us about the Tonton Macoutes, also terrifying, that they made unwanted people disappear. They weren't active anymore, but Dan didn't tell us that, and in any case, they still lived in imaginations—the henchmen, private militia of Papa Doc who worked to keep him in power. They were named for a Creole myth about "Uncle Tonton," who captures bad children and eats them for breakfast. There was so much I didn't know about Haiti's history: the only Caribbean island to successfully revolt against occupation, that they had to pay a ransom for their freedom that left them miserably in debt. I didn't know the history but could see clear as day that the police with their AK-47s were everywhere. I worried they were the Tonton Macoutes, ready to eat children for breakfast.

We returned home with crates of paintings, artists with names like Duval, Duffaut, Sassoon, Casimir, Blanchard.

Cathy was a little woman with a big stomach and a bright smile and laugh. She wore strappy sandals and a lot of gold, and though she was Dan's business partner, her role wasn't always clear in the conversations with the artists or the gallerist. My mother, she didn't seem to care about any of it—Cathy's role or the art. Mom carried baby Joan on her hip and took pictures of us endlessly on her Rolleiflex. She and Dan a few years before, after the birth of Joan, had come to Haiti to marry at the Hotel Oloffson and then have their honeymoon hiking Pic la Selle.

BACK IN NEW JERSEY, the furnace was still broken, and the taxman lurked at the bottom of the driveway. At some point the gallery folded and Cathy moved away. Dan started the raspberry farm with a local farmer and a sister's rich boyfriend. Dan sold pints of fresh-picked raspberries to local restaurants and to some restaurants in New York City as well, driving in to peddle the berries door-to-door, spending the money he made at bars. Once he got so drunk, he lost his car.

He continued seeing his patients, an odd collection of people—a woman who wet her pants, twin Sikhs, a nun. On weekends sometimes he would have workshops, send us kids away, and explore dolphin therapy in the swimming pool—which did not involve an actual dolphin. (It is likely, too, that I misunderstood where the dolphin therapy was taking place, but it seemed to my child's mind that it was happening in our swimming pool.) Always, Dan kept an office and always he had a book or an article he was working on that, when finished, would solve all our money problems. He was working on the definitive treatise on the psychology of love. His motto was "If a thing is worth doing, it's worth doing badly." He smoked a lot of weed and drank beer and wine and went to the opera and the symphony, and clipped things out of newspapers and magazines, articles and photographs. In those days, if you bought four six packs of beer, the liquor store would give you a cardboard "bottom." You could use these "bottoms" to organize your clippings and photographs. You could walk downstairs into the basement as my husband once did, soon after meeting me and before Dan died, and see the results of a lifelong project: a basement where every flat surface, every desk, every shelf, every piece of furniture, including the Ping-Pong table, was covered with cardboard "bottoms" stacked on top of each other, in great tiers, a towering hoard, a maze, a Lost City with each cardboard tier filled with a different category of clipping and following some invisible, obsessive, Casaubon-like "Key to All Mythologies" pattern with no visible organization. His clippings were cut from just about anywhere and depicted images of women belittling men.

"It was one of the scariest things I've ever seen," Mark said. "There was no way he was ever going to finish that project." Yet Dan toiled his entire life on it, becoming increasingly unhinged the closer he got to the end, when the Lost City in the basement became a clippings repository for unresolved issues with one's mother. In one such clipping, for what Dan called his "gynocracy collages," a group of four Victorian-era women peer with Olympian disinterest through a magnifying glass at a tiny, well-dressed man on his knees, his arms beseeching them to hold off on what looks, for all the world, like the beginning of a cold and calculated lab dissection.

NOW HERE I WAS at Omega Farm, my stepfather long dead, my mother vanished into dementia, my sisters busy and hunkered down, Elsewhere, while I, in a perpetual "workday," tried to fix the present, the underworld of memory making itself known, in its own way—here and there, in every piece of junk found in the woods, and in every patch-job and jerry-rigged "solution" from the broken, yet widening, spell of the past.

Out in the wider world, a grimmer reckoning reminded me to take stock and count my many blessings. Against that backdrop of bewilderment, I was, indeed, fortunate to be living in a broken-down house, distracted by home repairs, together with my family, worrying for them, how strange their world had become, and trying to keep my students on task in a class I was teaching on keeping a journal. Not a worst case, nothing heroic about that, but we are where we find ourselves, as Camus might have said in *The Plague*, a book that was back in heavy rotation along with *The Decameron*. After that, it's on you. The choices are to act with courage and good faith, or to begin a slow retreat behind the many facades of compromise, yet each exclusionary clause, each hastily scribbled addendum in the private contract one keeps with one's principles—each exception granted to oneself—still redounds to you.

Well, yes. It does. And it doesn't. It's complicated. Most of us, in our own way, some more than others, met the moment.

Our new circumstances in New Jersey involved roommates: my mother and Dayana. Her son, Juanpa, would come later from Colombia, in September of 2020, his trip delayed by the world closing down. Dayana had been with Mom for only six weeks when we moved in. Before that, she knew me, or a sister, only as weekend relief, coming out from the city to give her time off. She was young and gentle, had never cared for an ailing elderly person before, but you wouldn't have known it. Mom responded to Dayana's calm manner, and we all felt fortunate to have found her. I was there to give more help to Dayana, since she could not leave on the weekends to visit her mother in Queens. Apart from her days off, there were also moments in the day when I could step in when Mom became defiant, which happens with dementia.

I had my own fantasy to help me through the days, one I wasn't even completely aware of but that looked a little like this: I had my children back. We were here together in New Jersey, able to live out a rural version of our lives that I had sometimes wondered about, an alternate life, a parallel life, in which Mark and I raised our children in the country. I had once started and then put aside a novel about a mother who is sick of what is happening to her family, the widening separation created by the teenage years and the fast pace of New York City, the struggle to keep up with the Joneses, so she quits it all to become a flower farmer in rural New Jersey, towing her family along. A fantasy, yes, but here we were. And here, too, my kids on the precipice of adulthood, I could regain some time with them, make up for the parenting mistakes that I had made. I could also correct my own past, however such a thing might be achieved, though I had no idea what this meant or looked like or even that it was what I wanted—just an intuitive sense that

that was what one did when one went home again. Certainly, I was trying to fix things.

My daughter had recently turned twenty, a sophomore in college. In no other circumstance would she have come home in this way, moved into the bedroom that, when I was young, was shared by two of my stepbrothers. She made it hers, strung up fairy lights, collaged the walls with snapshots of her friends, moved the bed around, put her name on the door. She had fun exploring the house. In my mother's closet, in the basement, she found old dresses and made us dress up for dinners, for Easter, for a Norwegian smorgasbord she cooked herself. She dressed up Mom, cajoled Dayana into dressing up, too. We were "thrifting" at the Farm, as Livia liked to say. In the kitchen, she tended the chicks. On the deck she set up a salon and cut all our hair, including the tight curls of Gigi, our dog.

For my son it wasn't so easy. Two concussions had knocked him out of his freshman year of high school and now the pandemic had knocked him out of his sophomore year. He'd recently discovered the vast social network of his city life, had helped lead his basketball team to win a championship game. Down by eleven points, forty-five seconds left on the clock, he was brought off the bench, made a three-point shot, and then had a steal that led to another three-point shot and the momentum was theirs. He was a gregarious kid who made friends easily, had a girlfriend he was in love with. But he was stuck in New Jersey, on a farm, miles and miles of nothing. He didn't claim a room. He sat in the basement and played Xbox. When he emerged, he was hungry and angry, every inch of sixteen.

* * *

IN THOSE EARLY WEEKS, the trees still bare from winter, Livia and Jasper ventured into the forest. They went for long hikes on trails meandering for miles. When my mother put her land in the D&R Greenway Land Trust, she encouraged her neighbors to do the same, thus multiplying the extent of the preserved land. From the first hike, Livia and Jasper returned enchanted. "Why didn't you ever take us on hikes when we were kids?" my daughter asked. I said nothing—that I wasn't Thoreau wouldn't have been an explanation. Perhaps getting to know the forest, explore it, was a commitment to the place I had never been willing to make. Perhaps the forest scared me. Forests can be scary.

But my fantasy: I had my children back again. They were under a single roof in an alternate domestic universe in which I got to mother them all over again, but better this time because of what I'd learned: that time passes far too fast. Yes, yes, we all know that, but even so it is a shock, over before you can reckon with what needs to be reckoned with. I wouldn't yell at my children. I wouldn't be distracted by work and worry. I wouldn't be anxious and fearful. Instead, I made bread. I made pizza. I made fancy dinners from the *New York Times.* Sometimes Dayana would cook a fancy Colombian dinner. In the evenings, we put on Frank Sinatra for my mother, who was transformed by the music, came to life again. She liked to dance with my husband. For the moment, this house would be better for my children than it had been for me as a child, more ordered, more efficient, less chaotic. We drove on the empty roads to the garden supply center, an essential service (as was the liquor store, liquor sales being off the charts everywhere), we donned our masks and bought eggplants and peppers and tomatoes and okra for the garden, a mass of herbs, an heirloom rose bush, a fig tree. We could become, if not a country family, a family we hadn't been before, and that family would overwrite the family that had found itself shipwrecked here so long ago.

THE NEIGHBORHOOD HAD CHANGED a little. Our closest neighbors, the Viecelis, had sold their house to a young couple who rode dirt bikes at sunset, the engines buzzing across the golden hour. They'd put up big signs, warning of dogs, cautioning intruders to stay out. The Viecelis had been friendly in an odd way, had lived there for as long as I could remember, a family of four. Mr. Vieceli was Italian, had brass knuckles that he liked to show off to us kids when we wandered down the driveway to his house—a little guy, all muscle and ferocity behind an easy smile. We had a problem with a chicken once. It was injured, but still alive and suffering. Mr. Vieceli came over and with his bare hands twisted off the neck, decapitating the bird, which sprayed blood, clucking about for a moment then toppling over. When the job was done, he wiped his bloodied hand across his mouth. On another occasion, he roared up to our house in his white Lincoln to fetch his dog who had strayed into our garden where my mother was weeding. He pulled out a gun and shot at the dog, just grazing its head. Mr. Vieceli picked the dog up, shoved it into the back seat of his car, and tore off.

Mrs. Vieceli was French, petite, with a thick French accent that made her beautiful. She wore her long dark hair swirled on top of her head. At some point when we were kids, Dan had the notion that she should be our cook. We had no money, but she became our cook, cooking elaborate French meals for the twelve of us, then walking the long driveway home in stilettos. The idea of the cook was a remnant of Dan's life with Sally. Each of their children had been born in a different country. My stepbrother Danny, the oldest, boasted that he was African, since he'd been born there.

At some point the Viecelis' two sons grew up and Mrs. Vieceli moved to Las Vegas, leaving Mr. Vieceli alone down the road, where he quietly lived out the rest of his life until, at ninety-four, he pulled his car out onto Route 31 into the path of an oncoming tractor-trailer rig barreling down the highway and was killed instantly. The brass-knuckled neighbor who held down one corner of the map we all made back then met his angry end, and his house—the Vieceli house—was sold to the dirt bike riders, who annoyed me as I weeded our garden.

My fantasy was not my children's fantasy, or at least not my son's. After a month of this he couldn't take it. He'd explode one minute then disappear to the Xbox; occasionally Livia would cajole him into a hike.

"I've got a plan," he announced one evening. His girlfriend's family, of many means, had offered to send a jet to pick him up and bring him to their country house on Long Island, in Southampton. We could hardly afford our car payments. "What?" I said. And he explained again that they'd send a jet to a private airport near Trenton—just down the road. (Later, when I would recount this story, he would correct me: "Mom, it was not a jet. It was a little prop plane, and they were on their way to pick up some of their other children in Delaware." So be it.)

"You don't want to be that person," I answered. I hardly knew the girlfriend. Eventually, she'd come visit. A lovely, beautiful girl who showed up chauffeured in a black SUV, a little toy poodle peeking out of her purse, lots of gold jewelry that she'd take off when it bothered her and leave lying around here and there. "We should sell it," my daughter joked. "She won't notice."

"What kind of person?" my son asked.

"The kind of person who thinks he's above the lockdown, who believes he can do as he pleases and that the rules don't apply to him." I reminded him that there was a pandemic, that the country, the world, was sheltering in place, that that's what we were doing here.

In an instant we were fighting. It was nighttime and we were in Dan's study, where Mark had lit a fire. The fireplace in the living room was broken, had been for some years, too expensive to fix. The study was where Dan had seen his patients. It was lined with books—poetry, history, philosophy, feminism. Giant painted wood chess pieces looked down on us from one of the ceiling's beams. I can't remember the specifics of the fight. We weren't a full month into the pandemic, but we'd all had it. Suddenly. Like an unexpected explosion. I recall only words, shards: *toxic, depressing, miserable.* My husband was there but it felt like all the anger was directed at me. "This place isn't ours," the children shouted. I was forcing them to live here, and the pandemic was my fault. I was deep inside the chaos of my own childhood, and I had dragged my children with me. So much had happened in this room. It was swirling around me. Dan had had a family meeting, called us all together to tell us that Mom and my sisters and I would be moving permanently to the Farm. I was scared by this notion, my home, Drake's Corner Road, vanishing from my grasp. We also gathered in the study to choose the baby's name even though he'd already chosen it, Mom enormously pregnant. The baby would be named Joan for Joan of Arc. Among the books that lined the walls there was a small figure of Joan of Arc with her shield.

Outside, the death toll climbed.

Inside, we were yelling at one another.

"I hate you all," I said to my children and my husband. Oh, in that moment I did. I could feel it, a familiar anger swelling within me, that had an easy way of taking me over completely. A clobbering swirl of static in my head, beating around in there like a windstorm.

After giving birth to Livia, I had postpartum depression. All I could think about was that I'd given birth to death. A year passed before I would accept that I was depressed. When I finally sought help, the doctor said that my emotions weren't abnormal; we just don't speak enough about them. He had me consider nursery rhymes, fairy tales, bedtime stories. He recited "Rock-a-bye Baby," which bears repeating here:

Rock-a-bye baby, in the treetop
When the wind blows, the cradle will rock
When the bough breaks, the cradle will fall
And down will come baby, cradle and all

"That's a lullaby," the doctor said. *Lullaby* is defined as a quiet, gentle song sung to send a child to sleep. "If there weren't ambivalence, if childrearing weren't hard and scary, all these lullabies wouldn't have children dying in them."

Motherhood: everything is the mother's fault, she is to blame, she did something wrong to make her child's life the misery that it is. But motherhood: we are to be calm, guiding, inspiring lives, the inspiration behind the masterpiece. Motherhood: selflessness, needs erased or ignored; desires put on hold; longings deferred or annihilated while we make little lives perfect.

When my children were seven and three, I was asked by a magazine to go to Morocco for two weeks to write a story on a chef there. I said I could go for only five days; I had children. When I got off the plane, breathed the air, I called my editor to say that I could stay the full two weeks. On one of the last nights, I was in Marrakesh on the rooftop of a fancy hotel. It was late at night. I couldn't sleep. I was up there in my nightgown looking at the stars, so close it seemed you could pluck them from the sky, a North African breeze blowing lightly against my skin. I never wanted to go home. I wanted to stay there, alone.

* * *

ALL THESE YEARS LATER, we were in the study fighting and I wished I could get away and stop being responsible for everything, absolutely everything. I was mad, furious. An unspeakable rage born of helplessness, of not being heard or seen. I felt possessed, an ancient familiar sensation of not being heard. I had dragged my kids into my mess, my past, and I was mad at them for not better embracing it with me, for not making it perfect with me, that Jasper wanted to fly away in a jet. So much for parenting better. I grabbed my purse, got in the car, and stormed off into the night.

"Watch out," my sister Laura had said. "The Farm will eat you alive." It was something about the room, the books, the memories. The kids yelling at me, with no idea about the underworld of memories. By comparison, they had no memories, or at least they weren't living on top of them. And certainly, they didn't know about mine— of being locked inside the windstorm, wanting to get away from it. My husband said nothing. Husbands everywhere always seem to say nothing.

On the road, I thought of my mother, of being in our old green station wagon with her, my older sisters and me, Joan back at home in her crib, my mother trying to figure out if she should leave Dan or not. I was so young, eight, nine years old. Quietly I had hoped that we could just return to our big white house on Drake's Corner Road. But we couldn't. When we moved to the Farm, my father and Yolanda and her four kids moved into our house. They lived there now. They had bought out Mom's half and Yolanda's kids had moved into our old rooms. We drove around and around that night and I wished, I longed, that we could go home again.

THAT PANDEMIC NIGHT OF the fight, in truth, I had nowhere to go. I'd had a third of a bottle of wine. (Alcohol sales were up.) I drove to the nearest gas station and parked by the air pumps because one of our tires was low, but I had no quarters to fill it up. I called a friend and cried and told her I hated my family—knowing that that was not the truth. I loved them so desperately, too desperately perhaps. I wanted so much for their lives to be all that mine had not been. I wanted them to have that alternative life that I hadn't lived, the one in which my parents had stayed together, and I was confident and pretty. I wanted them to have everything I hadn't had and therefore I wanted to give them everything I possibly could and even more than I responsibly was able to. But it was a losing proposition, and I was failing. Patiently my friend listened. I'm trapped, I told her. Every day I watched my mother die a little bit more, her language leaving her word by word. We were being watched, observed, by Dayana, the caregiver. Though she didn't appear judgmental, she heard these fights. I didn't like the family we appeared to be with these fights. Jasper tried calling, but I refused to answer. I vowed to stay there until my son had passed through his teenage years and the world had gotten sane again, but a policeman who'd been watching me from his cruiser approached the car and told me that I might not realize it, being from New York (he had searched my plates and knew all about me), but that New Jersey was on twenty-four-hour lockdown. Only essential workers were allowed on the road. None of this was hardship. Hating your family wasn't hardship. Having a son whose girlfriend's mom offered to fly him in a private plane to the Hamptons—that certainly wasn't a hardship. It was weird. It was completely out of any human scale I knew. It was impossible to explain to a sixteen-year-old that it was wrong for someone to have so much money that they'd become disconnected from the human condition, when we ourselves, as our son would say, were not dissimilarly disconnected. I had a job. My husband had a job. We'd all had dinner. I'd had some rather nice wine. I'd driven while possibly drunk to a gas station to wait it out and the cop at the gas station hadn't decided to shoot me. Nor would he decide to shoot my husband when I finally called for a ride. Mark, in the fullness of a privilege he could deploy in a tight situation, rolled his eyes skyward and said to the cop, "It's been a night."

"Tell me about it," the cop said.

And then we drove home in silence.

WHEN I RETURNED TO the Farm, Jasper was crying. "I don't have a room here," he said. Right. The tears were real. None of this was hardship. In the morning, I cleaned every single book in the bookcases in Dan's study, dusting them, vacuuming them, removing cobwebs and mouse poop and dead spiders and cave crickets. The study gleamed. I brought up a bed from the basement, making a room for Jasper.

M y journal-writing class logged into an online platform that we called a "classroom," from whatever part of the world we found ourselves occupying—whatever dorm room closet, or basement workbench, or bedroom we could find on the fly, as each of us, student and professor, by the tens of thousands across the country, tried to assume the roles and fulfill the obligations we had accepted in the Before Times. A pandemic had locked us all into a unique and historic societal separateness, an on-screen spectatorship emerging for all of us who weren't first responders, who weren't paramedics, who weren't nurses and doctors working double shifts in hospitals, who weren't in-person schoolteachers, grocery store clerks, or, in that first summer of entanglement, who weren't out in the streets, or being pepper-sprayed, or shot at, or killed. Those of us who were left, instead, to ourselves and our syllabi, our classroom patter interrupted by barking dogs and lost Wi-Fi connections, watched the spectacle of a world coming slowly unglued from its foundational moorings. In that isolation, we could think about our choices, what we could do about any of it, and what the point might be, what exigence, what imperative there might be, to not just watch the spectacle but—no matter where and how and in what condition, good or ill, privileged or not—*to write it down,* to take notes about the spectacle, from whatever point of view one witnessed it, and to do this, faithfully, in a journal.

THE ACT OF WITNESS implicit in a journal is not just *reactive*: not just to say that this or that happened—in the very same way that a story is not, strangely, *what happens* in a story. A story is about something. That something is us—us, and what is the same about us, despite our separate circumstances and differences. These were the topics we discussed and that I came to think about more and more as I conceived this book. If I was going to account for my time during a plague, that account—again, strangely—would not merely be about me, or my family, or my mother's dementia, or how I planted sod and spread grass seed and repaired fences, grew a garden and raised chickens. Yes, it would be about those things but, no—it would have to be about more than those things.

THE PATH TO HIGHER reckoning for me, during this year, arrived obliquely, starting in early summer with a text from Bill, a tenant, who lives in the lower cottage of the two cottages. His electric meter, he wrote to me, was close to impossible to read and his oil tank was hard to access because of the bamboo growing over it.

When my mother's dementia became apparent in 2012, she was working full-time at her studio in Princeton, her schedule as packed as ever, but she missed appointments, had started racking up debt, took out a loan against the Farm to support the bills for the business. My sister Sarah, an art historian, a Bernini scholar, teaching at Emory, took over. Mom was close to $200,000 in debt. Sarah closed the business, moved Mom's studio to the Farm, took over all the bills, "scrubbed" her accounts, closed her credit cards, sorted out her taxes and everything else, became Power of Attorney, and watched over the Farm, and Mom, like a hawk from the bird's-eye view of Atlanta. We had a caretaker for the property, a guy who came to America from Honduras when he was fifteen, though we only learned that much later. He told everyone he was twenty-one. For years, it seemed, he was twenty-one. Mom took him on like all the strangers who came before to help and fix. Following suit, he stayed for years, and when he left, it wasn't a good parting, as they never seemed to be. Sarah had relied on him to do the work that needed to be done on the ground. He left shortly before the pandemic and here I was, in some ways his replacement.

I told Sarah about the bamboo. "I know all about the bamboo," she said from Atlanta over the phone. "You need to chop it down and then put Roundup in the culm."

The cottages, part of the long-ago hunting compound, are close to the house, separated only by the top of our driveway, where we park our cars. I could see the cottages from the kitchen window. I looked out at them now. We had always called them the "lower" cottage and the "upper" cottage because of the short hill that separates them. When we were young, they were occupied first by the big kids and their friends, but as we needed money, they became occupied by tenants. One of the first tenants was a man who played the synthesizer. He invited all of us to a show he was doing with Jefferson Starship in New York City. We piled into the Cadillac as we often did, the whole lot of us, and went to the show to watch Grace Slick sing about pills making you smaller and bigger and to hear our tenant play his music. We were seated next to Mick Jagger.

After the musician came a journalist to live in the lower cottage. Her name was Madeleine Blais and I remember that she was beautiful, and I loved her—kind and gentle. She had a boyfriend who wrote for *People* magazine, just launching, an offshoot of *Life* magazine.

In those days, 1975, Dan had a reputation for many things, one of which was that he was a househusband. He stayed home and took care of the kids while my mother went to work. Madeleine's boyfriend decided to profile Dan and Mom, us. At some point that year, there we were in *People* magazine, all of us, Dan sweeping the kitchen floor, a portrait of us seated on the sprawling, tiered front deck (the remains of which are junked in the woods), the kids on the driveway filling potholes, Mom in her studio looking at her work. On the cover of the issue of *People* was Marlon Brando. He looked so much like Dan we all thought it was Dan. For a moment we felt famous.

So many tenants came and went—a woman named Naomi, her husband's name was Stefan, pronounced with a long *a*. She gave birth to a baby in the cottage. Stefan grew pot in a second field that we had, the lower field, hidden by the trees in the forest. There was the roller-skating star who dreamed of being Wonder Woman but was married to a sad, fat little man, her roller-skating coach. On more than one occasion she gave me speed and made passes at me—I was a teenager by then. She had a girlfriend visit when her husband wasn't around. He developed liver cancer. On the day he died, his wife was off skating or with her girlfriend, so he called Dan and Dan went to the cottage to help him die.

Now, when I looked out the kitchen window, across the driveway, between the two cottages, I could see there might be a problem with the bamboo. I had always known the bamboo was there, but I had never *paid attention* to it. It had never been my concern, but now Sarah was asking me to get a machete and chop some of it down and poison it with an herbicide that was in the news for killing people. So I walked across the driveway and tried to take it all in. I watched the wind play against the bamboo, planted in a moment of whimsy years ago—because peacocks, I had been told, like to eat it and Dan had peacocks. I was also told that my mother had it planted in order to create a screen of privacy and to hide an ugly oil tank from view. In any case, the bamboo had grown into a green forest wall so thick you couldn't fit your hand into it, a bamboo fortress of green shadows— an impenetrable colossus. Impossible to know what might live in there. Maybe snakes, slaloming the tightly packed stand.

I searched the internet. A few days later a man from New Jersey Bamboo arrived with a clipboard. He walked the length of the bamboo stand, between and behind and around the two cottages and into the forest. The bamboo covered about an acre and a half. The estimate he sent to me for its removal was $100,000, but he couldn't even do the job. It was too big for his company. I got a similar estimate from a guy named Bamboo Bob, $80,000. Working my way down a list, I got a visit from an Italian junk removal man who also did odd jobs and liked the look of this one but didn't know what he'd do with all the bamboo culms. He suggested I start a vineyard in the field and offered to build me a pizza oven for $1,000. He spoke in Italian the entire time, which made me sort of love his idea and forget the bamboo for a moment. I had learned Italian when I was sixteen and it had sparked a curiosity in me that had heretofore been latent. Learning Italian made me want to learn about everything to do with the country and then beyond. The language saved my academic life, transforming me from a D student with few college options into an A student—a story my father loves to tell.

I settled on a guy named Anthony. I had also found him on the internet—the year before. He'd come to take down a cherry tree near the pool. Its roots had been pushing into the concrete walls of the pool, compromising it. Sarah had said that the tree needed to go. It was a weeping cherry planted when we first came to the Farm. That once-tiny tree had buckled the bricks of the pool deck. Anthony stood to make a few bucks taking down the tree, but he said the most it needed was a deep pruning of the roots. "It's a beautiful tree, a healthy tree." He spared the tree. The weeping cherry still thrives.

He looked the bamboo over and offered to clear it, the rhizomes, and the root balls for $7,500. Two dead ash that towered above the lower cottage, threatening to fall on it, he'd take down for another

$3,000. "I'll have to climb them," he explained of the dead ash. He had dark hair and a round friendly face, and dressed comfortably in clothes that seemed suited for shimmying up very tall trees. The ash trees were too close to the cottage, their limbs completely bare of leaves, scars streaking the bark. "It's the borer," he said. "They're all gonna die." He pointed to other ash looming above the bamboo and then to several more in our yard.

"The what?" I asked.

"The emerald ash borer," he said. "They're killing all the ash, all across the country." He pointed again to the trees, trees that all looked the same to me: healthy, skyscraper-tall trees with gorgeous, expansive canopies that had been shading our hill for centuries. A tree specialist once came to the Farm to look at some limbs that needed pruning. I was only half paying attention as I walked around the house with him and my sister Sarah—the boss, as I liked to call her, though she hated that. The certified tree specialist had given us a hefty quote for the limb removal, which we had not been able to afford, but he was full of admiration for what he saw.

"Monster trees," he said, looking up, his head tilted all the way back. "They're pre–Revolutionary War, I'd imagine, and this forest of yours has never been felled." According to him the "monster" trees were some four hundred years old. I understood nothing then about our trees, but I thought of the ancient redwoods and sequoias, the records, the knowledge they kept, and their age seemed like a good thing, *never been felled* seemed like a very good thing. I'd been proud of Mom's forest and the soaring oak and ash above the house.

I remembered Dan's stories of the Lenape, of George Washington camping at the foot of our driveway, and it all made a certain sense. We lived inside a forest where time stretched beyond the historical vantage point. These trees had seen a thing or two.

To Anthony I said, of the ash that weren't dead, "They look healthy. Look at all their leaves." They were beautiful trees, like champagne flutes.

"Next year there'll be fewer leaves. The year after next, they'll be dead, towering twigs."

I thought about the tree I had removed when I first got to the Farm, that the man pulled over with his little pickup racing across the lawn. I thought of the shattered crown and the hours we'd spent cleaning it up. It, too, had been an ash, killed by the borer. Learning about the borer, I could suddenly see their destruction, dying ash everywhere. We had ten ash in our yard alone. Though these were not dead, they would be soon, as Anthony said.

But right now, I was focused on the bamboo. Removing it, Anthony explained, would require heavy machinery, backhoes and excavators, so he'd need to know where the septic for the cottages was located.

As it happened, I had recently received a text from the tenant in the upper cottage reporting a septic smell and a gurgling in her toilet. Her name, too, was Sarah. On the night of the fight, she'd driven Mark to the gas station to pick me up. She had been Joan's best friend growing up and had lived in the upper cottage with her brother and mother for a couple of years as a child—others in the series of tenants. Her mother had been the first Delaware River-keeper and had overseen the cleaning of the toxic river, turning it into a healthy river that people could fish in and float on in inner tubes. She'd planted the enormous garden we still enjoyed. Sarah and Joan had gone to elementary school together down the road, starting in kindergarten, to the school Dayana's twelve-year-old son would attend in the fall, when the coronavirus would finally abate enough to allow flights from Colombia to resume.

Life had carried Sarah away and then recently back to Ringoes and into the cottage she'd lived in as a child. The back deck of the cottage pushed up against the bamboo grove. Next to both the deck and the wall of bamboo was a sludgy, bubbling, stinking hole that Sarah pointed out to me. Suddenly, it seemed, among other things, I had become a landlord by proxy.

The septic for the lower cottage was a mystery. I called the former caretaker. I called siblings. No one had any idea where the sewage for the lower cottage drained. Some suggested it was on the far side of the house, that it drained into the field that had once been filled with raspberries. That made sense.

I brought in a septic contractor from a company aptly named Stinky's, and showed him the smelly, gurgling hole near Sarah's deck. As it happened, she was on the deck doing yoga in a bikini. Together the three of us ventured to the edge of the bamboo to try to understand how the system might have been laid out, but the bamboo was too thick. He asked a bunch of questions. I made some more calls to the former caretaker and to a few sisters. Eventually the guy from

Stinky's said he'd need cameras and snakes in order to understand it. "But it's the rhizomes and root balls," he said. "They've got possession of the walls. They're going to cause a cave-in of what I'm guessing is an old cesspool." I was learning a lot of landlord stuff: in the timeline of sewage technologies, the cesspool was a Neolithic solution replaced by the more familiar septic tank and field. So ancient was the cottage cesspool, no one in the family knew that it existed or what happened to the sewage from the cottages. For fifty years, the toilets got flushed and nobody asked any questions.

"All that bamboo," the man from Stinky's said, "it's better if all of it goes."

When you scratch a problem like that, it becomes something else—a problem of history and entropy. *Something there is that doesn't love a cesspool.* Each separate problem pointed to a complicated, invisible, hyper-embedded set of interlinked and cascading problems, one thing piling upon another thing, and, worst of all, it involved something that we casually call *infrastructure*, the ugliest word in the English language and encompassing everything we like to hide away or bury in the ground so that we don't have to think about it too much. Problems with infrastructure present themselves in the way that the tip of an iceberg presents itself, the difference being that if you leave an iceberg alone, without an engineer or contractor standing next to you—dollar signs flashing in their eyes—it melts all by itself. But to fix the smell behind the cottages, to gain access to the oil tank, to be able to read the electric meter, I would need, first, to chop down an entire bamboo forest, which required heavy equipment and the biggest truck that had ever been driven up our gravel driveway, an eighteen-wheel thudding monster with a massive dumpster that shook the ground as it approached, with a stalky driver named Jason, partner of Anthony, who wore bib overalls without a shirt and backed up his big machine expertly, and drove off dozens of times with loads of shattered bamboo culms, and kept returning and driving off again even into the night as Anthony worked his backhoe yarding out the debris.

As I came to understand, even when cut down, bamboo shoots will pop up once again as fast as you can say *invasive species*. The rhizomes and the root balls needed to be removed, too. But those roots grabbed and held on to rocks and anything they could clutch like talons, intractable—each root ball a hard-ridged, obdurate concentrated, and evolutionarily focused hub of refusal and resistance that said *No* to any force in nature that might try to yank it from the ground, that said to anyone who might wander by with a pickax, for instance, and a mind to remove a rhizome or two: *fuck you, fuck you*. And, indeed, when all the bamboo was cut down and the last dumpster loads got hauled off, the sunlight slanting on the cleared land behind the cabins, an entirely new acre or two of New Jersey lay reclaimed, but you could see the rhizomes shining like a thousand rivets in the ground. They weren't going anywhere.

Bamboo, I realized, is just about the worst thing anyone could ever decide to plant anywhere, for any reason. Even garbage dumps don't want to have anything to do with bamboo. When I asked Jason, the stocky truck driver, the one with the giant dumpster, where he was hauling the mountain of bamboo, he demurred and pointed to another guy Anthony had brought on to operate one of the backhoes. That guy pretended not to hear me, and then pointed to Anthony. When I asked Anthony where they were dumping the bamboo, he laughed and changed the subject. Dumping bamboo, it seemed, was the arboreal equivalent of the guy who gets whacked in a mob movie. We all know it happens, but where it gets dumped is a subject best left to the professionals.

THE LITTLE UNINCORPORATED COMMUNITY where Omega Farm is located has been known as Rocktown for some 175 years. A highly wound, aspiring gentleman farmer from somewhere in suburban New Jersey, who bought the farm at the foot of our hill very recently in a foreclosure sale, told me in conversation that the Rockefellers were the namesake of the area, that a Rockefeller was buried in the cemetery at Sandy Ridge just down the road. He'd studied the local history before buying the place. I had grown up here, had heard many stories, but had never heard about the Rockefellers in Ringoes. Sure enough, a Rockefeller is buried in the cemetery there. But when I told this story to my father, a man known for factual accuracy, he said, "There are a lot of Rockefellers around these parts, a few different spellings, none have much to do with the Rockefellers you're thinking of." Whatever the case, in Rocktown there are a lot of rocks. If the rocks had value, we'd be wealthier than the Rockefellers.

My father's explanation for the name, which came only from intuition, involved the abundance of rocks. Some ten thousand years ago a glacier melted not too far from here. Pushing down from the north, it plowed quite a lot of debris. The glaciers had departed but the bamboo had latched on to the rocks and wasn't going to let go. I fact-checked the glacial spill with my father. "That is not what I said at all," he admonished. "The glacier of which you speak stopped some twenty or thirty miles from Rocktown. If you're going to write about geology, make sure you're accurate."

He said he would look into the rocks of Rocktown but didn't get back to me for several weeks. When finally he did, he explained that he'd been waiting to speak with a retired Princeton petrologist who came from California, has a town there named for his family, but whose entire career was made upon the rocks of the Sourland Mountains of which the Farm is a part—named Sourland long ago because the land was no good for farming.

"The rocks are autochthonous. That means they are in place, not brought from somewhere else like allochthonous rocks, rocks from elsewhere, carried by ice, glacier erratics." Dad went on to explain what he had learned from Linc, his geologist friend, using words like *diabase, argillite, ridges, sill*—intrusions between layers like the white part of an Oreo inside the black wafers. I took notes. Dad wanted to see samples of the rock. I love to hear my father speak about geology. It's hypnotic. But I can never remember accurately. The words and images swirl together into poetry. What I took away from this lesson was that the rocks of Rocktown were native and had broken down over the years because of weathering—water, freezing, thawing, the chemistry of which breaks apart the rocks.

He asked me to bring him the samples so that he could show them to Linc. He then added that Linc was colorblind and told me that many renowned geologists are colorblind, that being colorblind is helpful. "Color is misleading," Dad said. "For example, in the Grand Canyon the red wall limestone is not actually red. The rock above leaches into it." If you don't see color, you won't be confused. Then Dad added, "Just like you, stained from the rock above."

The next day Dad called me back. "I have ground rules," he said. "If you're going to write about geology, you need to show it to a geologist. I never show my work to the subjects before publication except with geology. You do not want to get it wrong."

"I'm listening, taking notes for the memoir," I said. "Your ground rules are more interesting than the geology."

"I've already written all of this in *Draft No. 4*."

"Of course you have," I said. I then asked him if he'd write up a few sentences about the rocks here at the Farm.

"What are you doing," he asked.

"Outsourcing," I said.

ANTHONY GOT FED UP with the rocks of Rocktown. He worried they'd bust his machines. Further, he discovered that there wasn't just one layer of rhizomes and root balls, but two, sometimes three.

Matters got worse before they got better. Better, in fact, seemed to be nowhere in sight. This was a bigger job than Anthony had realized. He gave up and I couldn't blame him. He'd ridiculously underbid the scope of a job more experienced professionals had understood. The $100,000 quote from New Jersey Bamboo flashed across my mind in neon. I felt sorry for Anthony. The culms gone, some of the root systems dug up, the area cleared, even more problems of entropy were revealed that had nothing to do with Anthony. The septic for the lower cottage was entirely busted, open, spilling from the house through pipes that had long ago been cracked, eaten by the bamboo. We now knew where the septic system was located, an ancient cesspool that had been feeding the bamboo, helping it to flourish for years.

"You're gonna need a new septic system for the cottages," Anthony said. He also discovered both a buried oil tank and one on the surface, tossed in the trees to get rid of it like all the other garbage. A buried oil tank is not a good thing, he told me. If it is leaking it can cost hundreds of thousands of dollars to clean up.

He took no pleasure in delivering all this bad news. It weighed on his face, brought his shoulders down. He felt sorry for me. Somehow all of this had become my problem; I had allowed it to become my problem. I have a tendency to believe that everything is my fault and that therefore I should fix it. But I didn't dwell on that; there was more. As promised, Anthony climbed the dead ash trees and limb by limb he brought them both down. Then he warned me about the ash surrounding the main house, how they die, eaten up from the inside until a storm blows through and knocks them down. "You've got to get rid of them," he said. There were eight ash looming above the main house and two by the pool—a lot of money, a lot of work cleaning up the splash.

Before leaving he suggested I buy industrial black plastic, enough to cover the area of bamboo rhizomes. "And just bake it," he said. "Cook it up."

My mother was inside coloring, her favorite pastime after sweeping, bathed and beautifully dressed by Dayana, who sat near her, working on the business she was starting as a life coach, the two of them side by side, deep in their work. Mom would smile when she saw me, ask me for a kiss. She was in there sitting at the dining table, oblivious to what was happening in the world, to the pandemic, to the election, to the Black Lives Matter protests, to the world blowing up and coming unhinged.

I knew where I was headed—down the rabbit hole. "Eaten alive," Laura had warned. Little shoots of bamboo were already popping up everywhere. The estimate for a new septic system came in at close to $20,000 and it had to be done, it was illegal not to do it, and as a result it had to be done immediately. Open sewage was not an option. There was no money for the job. "Sell it," all of my sisters, except for Sarah, said, from their perches in Elsewhere. I was jealous of them. "It's a sinkhole." Country houses were in high demand, the rich fleeing the city, real estate values soaring. But they knew as well as I did that selling wasn't an option. "Sell it" had become a meaningless mantra that we all said from time to time over these long years of

Mom's dementia. But we didn't have the money for a care facility for Mom—one we would be comfortable putting her in. The sale of the Farm wouldn't have been enough to cover the cost of a home if she lived beyond a few years. Even so, we could tirelessly threaten and speculate and throw up our hands while trying to figure out what to do. Where would Mom go? We could go round and round and round this question, the question working its way into our own relationships, taking its toll. Each of us had our own notion about what should be done, though really there was no choice here.

The Farm, with its main house and its outbuildings and barns, was an organism, alive though sinking into the woods, into a cesspool, and I felt completely overmatched by its many demands. Like my stepfather before me, I searched for ideas that would bring in some extra cash—a little income to keep the forest at bay. Mark mentioned growing cannabis, the laws of New Jersey about to change in the November election, making it legal. Livia and Jasper liked the notion of their parents becoming cannabis farmers. They were still with us full-time, the pandemic still very much alive in this summer of 2020. Livia had started a nonprofit called Fund the Revolution to raise money for entities associated with Black Lives Matter. She did this by selling used clothes that friends and family donated to her. She was very busy, raised some $3,000, cajoled Jasper to help her with all the mailings. Meanwhile, Mark and I did think that we could become farmers. Perhaps we could grow Christmas trees. I made calls to see if any local farmers were interested in growing alfalfa in our field. But really what I did was cry, for a long, long time. I was wrestling the Farm. I was down. The Farm was winning. Why was I doing this? I could leave. I had a home. I could take my kids and go back to New York City, go back to my life, to my home, ignore the problems as I had for a lifetime. This was not my home, as my son liked to remind me. I, too, could be Elsewhere.

But, of course, I could not. Returning home at this point would mean abandoning my mother and Dayana, as visiting still wasn't possible because of the virus. You were either in or you were out. There was no middle ground. No part of me could do that. When I took groceries to my father, I left them outside, waving to him and my stepmother through the window, all three of us masked.

MOST OF MY LIFE, it seems to me, I've been trying to put my family back together, to understand it, gain mastery over it, fix it. I was four when my parents separated. Across my childhood I looked for signs that they were still in love, that they'd reunite. It didn't seem impossible. On what would have been their twentieth wedding anniversary, both remarried to others, my father gave my mother a book of wine routes in France. One they had traveled when Sarah and Laura were babies had been highlighted by Dad with a yellow highlighter. We'd heard the story of that trip so many times, how they dined in Michelin-starred restaurants, leaving the babies asleep in the car. In my kitchen in New York, I had a menu from one of these culinary excursions framed and hanging on the wall. Asterisks drawn by Dad indicated what dishes they had eaten, what wine they had drunk.

Sometimes I imagined who I'd have been had they not divorced—an entitled girl from Princeton, growing up in a big white house in the woods at the edge of town, confident in herself and her beauty. Sometimes I could see her, that other me—almost unrecognizable, living the life that could have been mine.

Shortly after we moved permanently to the Farm, Mom and Dan got into one of their fights. He found carousels of slides from Mom and Dad's life together with my sisters and me, our life as a family, Dad's love letters to Mom. In his rage, he dumped them in a heap in the driveway, squirted gasoline on the heap and lit a match. I remember Mom standing over the fire, the slides melting, staring with a big, blank expression, numb—the horror she must have felt. For me, the fire, the burning of our past, defined Dan's jealousy and that jealousy gave me hope.

MY MOTHER TOLD ME to keep a journal. "Take notes," she had said. "You have an interesting family." I was about ten, terrible in school. I couldn't concentrate. I worried about what was going on at home. School seemed entirely unimportant to me. At home, I could keep order, make plans. I learned to cook, and I was cooking for the table of twelve on a regular basis, learning to make complicated things like Chicken Kiev, Chicken Supreme, Angel Food Cake. Once I tried to make those croissants. We all had dinner jobs, all ten of us: Before Dinner and After Dinner. We ate so late, sometimes around ten p.m., Mom coming in with the camera bags hanging off her shoulders. I figured out that if I was Before Dinner, I could get to bed earlier. I was always tired, liked to go to bed earlier than the others. I learned that I liked to cook, that I could be done early with my job, but also there was pleasure in feeding people, taking care of them, a good feeling spreading over me when they enjoyed what I had made. The Chicken Kiev is pounded, thinned chicken breast formed as a ball filled with herbed butter, sealed, breaded then fried. If prepared properly, the butter fountains from the chicken when cut into. I loved to watch the surprise as the butter burst forth, felt proud, successful.

My father drove out to the Farm three days a week to drive my sisters and me to school. It was allowed in the divorce decree. On those days, I went to school, but for a long stretch on the other days I stayed home—long leisurely days, the house empty, Mom at work, Dan driving off somewhere to lose time. He'd come home with ducks, peacocks, a new notion of some kind or other, fruit trees to create an orchard. At home I cooked, and I also did what my mother said: I wrote things down. "Observe," she'd say to me. "Details," she'd say to me. She had wanted to be a writer, had started a children's book, had won an award from the state of New Jersey for the work, but life got in the way.

My first novel was about my family and then in one way or another so were the four that followed. In June of the first summer of the pandemic, when I was fighting the bamboo, I was also publishing my fifth novel, *An Elegant Woman*—about my grandmother's life. I'd clean off the day, try to make myself look presentable, and then hop onto a Zoom event to promote the book. The backdrop was the photographs of my ancestors, staring at the Zoom camera from the walls—characters from the novel: Glenna, my great-grandmother;

Grammy as a girl, as a nurse, a wife and sister and mother; my mother as a bride. Even I was on the wall, an ancestor already it seemed. We were all together, and somehow, I liked it. I didn't feel alone. It gave me something clear to speak about. In the novel, I hadn't changed the names of the characters from my grandmother's generation. Their history had been imparted to me by my grandmother through story-telling, so it was as good as fiction for me, fiction in its most expansive, able form. So, as such, I'd left their names alone. I had recently reread the Katherine Anne Porter short story "Old Mortality." At the end of it she describes the weight of the ancestors, feeling oppressed by them, wanting to escape them. I couldn't appreciate the sentiment. I wanted to hang on to them, live inside my grandmother's room, those opera capes of hers still in the closet. Getting rid of the past seemed just as insurmountable as going to school had as a kid. There was so much I didn't know or understand that, perhaps, started with my great-grandmother's decision to leave her husband in 1910, take her daughters west, leave them alone to raise themselves, creating in my grandmother a fierce desire to survive, which, when she was an adult, became a fierce desire *to arrive,* which created a trap for my mother—a beautiful girl bred to marry. When the marriage with my father fell apart, my mother seemed to renounce all convention. It was a flagrant denunciation of my grandmother's dreams for my mother. Dan drove into her life in that Cadillac, smoking a joint, wearing a cowboy hat and a half-cocked smile, dreams of romance and adventure. "He has a big imagination," she would say to us, her daughters. Where does anything begin and end?

I have written all about my family, but I have never written this:

First—

I DROVE TO MY father's house as I did every week across the pandemic. I food shopped for him so that he wouldn't risk his life, or my stepmother's, in the grocery store. They too were old; he was almost ninety. I had noticed a pickax in his garage, and today when I went to them, I asked if I could borrow it. "It's a pick mattock," he said and explained the difference, standing in the doorway, masked. I love my father's precision. He loaned me the pick mattock, and I took it back to the Farm and I went immediately into the bamboo forest, and I started hacking away at the root balls and the rhizomes myself. I used the pick side to make holes, to perforate the dirt gripping the root ball. I then used the flat side to connect the holes and loosen the ball, pry away the rocks. I was out there in the rain, in the heat, in my bikini, in my sundress, in shorts, in pants. I was out there every day. I employed my son to be out there with me. I involved my husband. I even got the tenant Bill, of the lower cottage, to help me. One by one I was going to remove every last rhizome and root ball—tear apart this once-upon-a-time whim: *put up a little bamboo to hide the ugly oil tank, give the cottages a little privacy, feed the peacocks.* I hacked away with a determination I can have. I was going to win. I was not going to lose. I was going to fix this. I worked until my arms were sore, my back was sore, for days that accumulated, turning into weeks. I hacked away with a physical strength I didn't know I had, with a vengeance, with violence even.

Now—

WHEN I WAS ELEVEN years old, I had a bad dream. It was about a bear. I remember that very well. I had likely recently returned from a canoe trip with my father. He took us on long canoe trips, my sister Jenny and me—to the Adirondacks, to the Algonquin Park in Canada. There were always stories of bears, people mauled to death. We strung our food up in baskets on elaborate pulley systems, so they were high in the branches of a tree, out of reach of the bears. One of the mauling stories haunted my dreams and I woke up afraid. I slipped out of my bed and went to my mother and Dan's room. Joan was about two, still in a crib in their room. I slipped into their bed, the way children do to find comfort when afraid. Mom and Dan still had the waterbed, which was set within a painted wood frame, sunshine yellow. There was a crevice where the waterbed met the frame. It also sloshed a bit when it was sat upon, and it sloshed now as I entered. I lay my head down and fell asleep.

I woke up to a sensation that was at first pleasant, my body rocking, swaying in an instinctual rhythm all its own. My stepfather was lying next to me. I could hear him breathe. One of his fingers was in my anus, moving around in there. At first, I didn't want this to stop. I am ashamed to say that, even now. I have never written that before.

As I became more aware, a terror creeped in—slowly yet steadily. Then an embarrassment. Then a fear. Then a desire not to make Dan feel bad if I escaped, as I thought about how I might leave the bed. I pretended to be asleep, to move in my sleep, adjusting my position so that his finger was disturbed, cramming my small body into the crevice where the waterbed met the frame. I was wide awake. I waited for a long time, wedged there in the crevice. This was a strategy, I was thinking on the fly, understanding already, at eleven years old, that I didn't want to make Dan feel bad, I didn't want him to feel embarrassed or rejected. I was trying to erase what happened—not for me, that was impossible. I was doing it for him. When I thought Dan had fallen back to sleep, I snuck away to my bed.

I CAN STILL FEEL the sensation of the shame, red and hot spreading from my heart. I can feel it in my chest, running the length of my arms to my fingertips, from the edges of my ears seeping across my face. I know what it feels like not to want to speak, not to know what to say, not to know what to think, feel, or believe. I knew that I should not say a word. How does a child know this? What prepares a child for this? Dan never told me not to speak. What happened when I saw him the next day? I cannot remember that. How did I know not to say anything to my sisters, my mother, my father, my friends? Shame. We live on planes; we can bury swiftly, stack up and build high, silo and compartmentalize, move on until the moment is smothered by time. But we all know it is not. I can see my children, my father, my sisters— do they need to hear this again, or for the first time? Do I need to be so graphic here? Can I speak in euphemism, as I have done in my novels? I see my nieces, my nephews. I see Dan's children. Do I have to use that word? I don't want to use it again, feel that part of me that doesn't want to speak, feel it constricting at my throat, its very own muscle. Do I have to mention how it felt? Do I need to do this to myself again? That shame persists. I'm not worried about my husband; he knows the shame intimately; it has been a constant companion in our marriage. When my father learned the gist of this story, there was nothing he could do as Dan was already dead.

Memory is weird. Perspective turns history into fiction. But the memory of this doesn't change. It remains exactly the same and I am still there, and I can't leave there by recalling it in a different way. There is no different way. The pleasure and the shame and the guilt, the desire to protect, the fear, wanting to be good. How I wanted to be good. I wanted to be good. I am a good person. "You say that a lot," a sister recently noted. We are there, Dan and I, in that room with my mother and my baby sister, in a waterbed frozen in time so we can never leave no matter how hard I try or how much I want to.

MY MOTHER WANTED US to love Dan. From the very beginning. She wanted us to see the magic side. His turquoise Cadillac. The poker winnings that he'd pin to our bedroom doors in the house on Drake's Corner Road on the nights after a win. The sense of adventure. The trips to Haiti, to Mexico—gliding down the Sierra Madre, our van out of gas, making it on empty to a gas station in Guadalajara, escaping catastrophe and banditos. "The things you're seeing," Mom would say, "while your friends back at home are going to Fire Island, same house, same place year after year." Dan was fighting for women's rights. We were a family, a new American family. We didn't follow the rules. We were unique, original. We cared about seeing and understanding the world, adventure and living. Adventure was the operative word. We weren't afraid to have heated debates about big topics. We were informed politically, on the right side of human rights, civil rights, women's rights. THIS AD INSULTS WOMEN. We invented our own path forward, Dan our charismatic leader. I loved saying to people that I had nine sisters and brothers, that we were ten in all. If I included Yolanda's kids (I loved them, love them, too, very much), we were fourteen in all. I believed in that, a good thing, so many people to love.

I HAD NO VOCABULARY to speak about what had happened between Dan and me. Is that even the correct way to formulate that sentence? "What happened to me"? Would that work better? I didn't try to find the words. It wasn't until later that I wondered if my mother had been awake on the other side of the bed, wondered if she had known. Had the sloshing waterbed disturbed her? Then I dismissed the thought, as she was a very deep sleeper, hard to wake in the mornings. It wasn't until even later that I told her, and she said to me, "Men do that." Her grandfather had done it to her. I stopped speaking to her for two years. I was a young woman, living in New York City.

It took some time, but eventually Dan came to see me to try to make things right. I was glad that he was coming. I loved Dan. I wanted Dan to love me, to see me as smart and beautiful. I felt ugly around him. Generally, I felt ugly. But somehow, I thought something could be said that would make me feel beautiful. He said he would arrive by lunch; he would take me for lunch, and we would speak. Lunch passed and then dinner passed. I started drinking vodka that I had in the freezer until I was just a little drunk.

Eight hours late, he arrived. We went to a pub around the corner from my apartment for beer and hamburgers. He began with an explanation for why he was late. He'd gone to a Francesco Clemente exhibit, an artist I had never heard of. The painter painted images of vaginas inside men's heads, penises inside women's hearts—that was what I took away from Dan's explanation. Somehow this artist, these images, delayed him by eight hours. Why did I need to know this? Why was he here and not my mother? Why wasn't my mother here? But I didn't ask that question at the time. I accepted that the job was Dan's to resolve. He made the mess; he needed to clean it up. He then began discussing men and art, how men had been glorifying women in art for centuries, but that women had not done the same, women had not glorified men in art. Women did not care about men. The Abbey Pub was dark, but I could still see his face; it seemed to shine, that half-cocked smile, his large forehead, receding hair. His big eyes calibrating how contrite to be versus how in charge. He was in charge of me, and he knew it. I engaged, made a counterargument regarding the fact that women hadn't had much of a place throughout most of art history. He listened and nodded, indicating I'd made a point, but we didn't discuss it further.

Many of these details I found only when I revised this manuscript after having let it sit for a year. I found the details in my diary from 1991. I have kept journals most of my life. I reread the passage, November 10, 1991. I lay in bed miserable waiting for Dan, who called several times to say he was delayed. I actually did not drink vodka (or if I did, I didn't write about it) but did have four beers with Dan at the pub, later chastising myself for drinking with him at all. Instead of drinking vodka, I was lying in bed reading *The Sound and the Fury*, which I was loving very much. At the end of the evening with Dan, I gave it to him because I wanted him to love me and think that I was smart. He had not read the novel. I chastise myself for giving him the novel that I hadn't yet finished and that I wanted to keep for my own bookshelf, it was a hardbound copy and it was mine and I gave it to him, almost as if required, a toll—another attempt to make him feel not bad but better.

What strikes me about the journal entry is that I don't name what happened even there, even in my most personal and direct conversation with myself, for fear of it being read, of this truth hurting the trespasser of my journal. "Dan came in to see me to talk about 'our problem.'"

We were there, sitting alone together in the pub, the Abbey Pub, where I went with friends from graduate school. I was at Columbia at the time. Sitting there I was still waiting for a revelation or at least to feel pretty. He continued, moving on from "Dicks in hearts" to tell me that "he had overcome his problem of young girls' breasts and it felt entirely liberating. He rambled for a good ten minutes about how great it felt, and I was certainly annoyed because I was far from over 'my problem.'"

Until rereading this journal entry, I had no recollection of his confession to me about overcoming his problem with young girls' breasts.

He spoke about something he'd seen on TV, electrodes attached to the heads of cabbages, how the cabbages reacted through the electrodes when they saw a woman approach with a knife. I was drinking the beer, not eating the hamburger, feeling a bit woozy and drunk and still waiting for something deep and impenetrable to lift inside of me, to be freed from something I still had no words for so that I could return to my mother, for that was the reason I was here. Dan was the route back to my mother.

He had big sparkling eyes, that half-cocked smile that invited you inside to listen to him. He took on a serious, concentrated tone and told me that when he lived in Paris a taxi driver had somehow tried to molest a little girl he was close to. By the time Dan understood what had happened, the taxi was gone. He told me he felt such a helpless rage, that if he could have, he would have killed the taxi driver. *Is helpless rage what happens to me when I become possessed with fury?* When this girl was about fifteen, she fell in love with a guy. Dan caught them having sex, got a shotgun, and chased the guy, naked, down the driveway—so the story goes.

I still didn't feel pretty. I felt apologetic, like I needed to let Dan know that what happened didn't matter. That I was okay, that worse things had happened to other people (that was my refrain and would be across the years), that I forgave him. It was all fine, I was fine, we could keep the family myth intact. "The miserable thing," I wrote, "is that nothing has changed. If anything has changed it's that he may feel a little better about himself."

Secrets. Secrets everywhere. How many secrets we were all carrying, of our own, of others, asked implicitly to keep them, hold them inside—so many layers of secrets, upon secrets, upon more secrets. You become numb. You lose your voice. You are afraid to speak. I did not inquire about Dan's problem with young girls' breasts. I could not even retain that he had said it. It was in my journal, but not in my memory.

THERE HAD BEEN ANOTHER time. I was sixteen. We'd had a Christmas party at the Farm, and I had gotten very drunk. My father was there and for some reason I was mad at him. I danced flirtatiously with Dan and then I led him away from the party to a mattress in the study, the room I had turned into Jasper's room during the pandemic, dusting off every single book, clearing away the mice droppings and the cobwebs. The room of our family fight, the night I ran away to the gas station. I led Dan into the book-lined study, the giant chess pieces watching us from the ceiling beam. We lay down together on the mattress while the party carried on. I woke up there alone in the morning, embarrassed, humiliated. For years I wondered if anything happened, but it hadn't; I was sixteen, ugly with braces; he wasn't interested in me; I was no longer a child.

Another thing Dan told me in the Abbey Pub that late night so long ago was that he had been molested by a neighbor when he was a child. He looked at me hard, with sympathy if not love. I still did not feel pretty. I felt ugly. Impossibly ugly. I don't think Dan was capable of loving me. He'd burned my family's slides, after all. But he said now, "The man lived just a few houses down from mine, but on my way home from school I could cross to the other side of the street. I didn't have to see him again. I could avoid him." He was emphatic in this point. "You couldn't avoid me, Babe. You had to walk by me every single day of your childhood."

When I was researching my second novel, *Gorgeous Lies*, I went to the street that Dan lived on as a child, I studied his home, and I studied the houses across the street, imagining in which one lived the man who had molested him.

Dan did not once, that night at the Abbey Pub, say that he was sorry.

LONG BEFORE #MeToo, I was aware that so many women I knew had been molested in one way or another. With the #MeToo movement,

it seemed that just about every woman had had some form of unwanted sexual advance. There was, if not comfort, a sense of not
being alone, that collectively there was a voice that could have a
chance of stopping this once and for all. But no matter how many
women share a similar experience, the processing of it can only be
done entirely alone in the very private moments of shame.

DURING THE PANDEMIC, I cleaned out the basement. In papers
there belonging to me, I found a letter from my mother from this
time in which I would not speak to her. "I wake up every morning
hoping this nightmare will have passed and that I will see the sun
shining and you'll be there." Now, she was upstairs, coloring, seated
in her spot at the dining table in the dining room overlooking the
lawn and fields, gone. But there was nothing more I needed to ask
her about this; I had long since forgiven her, if only because I could
not live my life without her. I did cry, though, for the swift stealthy
movements of time—for how we tumble through with our palette of
emotion, to be deposited in a chair with no record at all.

IN OUR TWENTIES, MY sisters and I found the vocabulary and we
started speaking about our childhoods. We compared notes. We
didn't stop talking about this subject for some ten years, it seemed.
I'm certain this overlapped with my estrangement from my mother,
my meeting with Dan at the Abbey Pub, but I don't recall how those

details intersected. It could be that the estrangement helped ignite the conversation, but in truth how it started is lost to me. What I recall is that we spoke and spoke and spoke. Early on we all lived near each other on the Upper West Side, "the McPhee ghetto" one of our cousins called it. How many dinners, how many runs and walks, and visits to the Farm, endless late nights—once I recall us all crammed into a small car on a street in the city, car alarms and sirens wailing now and then. We talked deep into the night, a relief for us to know that we shared a sense of the crazy, that what we had lived had happened to each of us in our own ways.

I'd been embarrassed to share my story, but eventually I did. Somewhere in here I earned the badge of having had it the worst. What Dan had done to me had been worse than what he had done to my sisters . . . or at least that's what my imperfect memory recalls. What does that even mean, *had it the worst*? But somehow and for some reason, that wasn't about pity, that's what I latched on to. None of us felt sorry for the others, just the relief of knowing the experience had been real. In fact, I sort of liked that I'd had it the worst. Funny, crazy thing to admit, but somehow the fact settled into a spot of weird longing—that I had been chosen by Dan and I wanted to have been chosen by Dan. Somehow, too, it gave me a focal point for pain and anxiety—an explanation for the turbulence I could feel, the reactive rage that could course through me uncontrollably, in charge of me.

But the truth, I think, was this: I was the youngest and most easily accessible—the only one who would still climb into the parental bed. One sister hightailed it out of the Farm as soon as she could. Another sister, I can still see Dan chasing her down the hall at the Farm, twelve or thirteen. It was a game. I can see his face, mischievous expression, all the other kids around. He caught her by the back of the shirt, which fell off as he tugged, leaving her chest bare. He grabbed her fingers and pressed them back until she said "Uncle." Lots of laughter. Even this sister laughed, game, a sport. On her bedroom door she screwed and drilled in thirteen locks. She had the key for each lock. The other sister, I don't know the details of her shame, but for a long time I thought she escaped because until she was about thirteen she didn't like to shower, wash her hair, or change her clothes. When we gathered on the waterbed as a family to watch *Upstairs, Downstairs*; *I, Claudius*; *Roots*, Dan made her sit on the floor away from the rest of us.

We talked and talked and talked some more. We thought that we understood, that we could head into our lives consciously. Actually, we knew nothing, or very little, or at least I knew very little. What can we ever know really about the depths of someone else's experience? In that car on the dark late-night Manhattan street, what did I really know about my sisters' childhoods and what really did they understand about mine?

SO, THERE I WAS, in a pandemic, in New Jersey, in my childhood home, fighting a colossal force of bamboo. With each rainstorm, with each hot summer day the spear-like sprouts of bamboo pushed through the rock dirt, and I was there with my pickax, my pick mattock, to greet it. But they kept on coming. That's when I realized that I'd become a rhizome. Something hard in me said no to that, to being a rhizome with their proliferating subterranean root systems, said no to being stuck and entrenched, unyieldingly rooted in the past. I was rooted in a problem, many problems—small and large and larger—but there had to be a way, a work-around, even if I couldn't see it yet.

THE SHAME OF DAN has haunted my marriage. The shame of Dan has made me feel like a freak, like I don't belong in certain social situations—alongside the parents of my children's friends, the fantasy being that they are well-adjusted and haven't been humiliated in the ways that I have been, that they are worthy, and I am not. The shame of Dan is a container for the shame of my childhood, the chaos and fear, the powerlessness, the anger. The freak in me is hiding a festering abscess, and though it is hidden in the deepest part of my chest, it is there for everyone to see. Something is wrong with Martha. I was broken and everyone could see it because I was no good at hiding it. But I was also excellent at pretending—for others and for myself. I could, I can be, many things at once.

In therapy with my daughter not so long ago, the therapist said that abuse was a family disease. It rippled across generations. I didn't like to hear this, the ugliness of this. I hated this therapist. Dan had been molested. My mother had been molested. Secrets become those abscesses that have a way of draining themselves, one way or another.

And there is baby Joan. Tall and beautiful. Extremely successful, with a wife and three beautiful daughters, a thriving career. All her life she glorified Dan. Dan had loved her perfectly. He indulged all her whims: a picnic on the blizzardy banks of the Delaware in January—why not? Of his six children she was the one he was going to get right. The rest of us understood that we were the supporting cast, that Joan needed to be protected, why should she suffer, that for this to succeed the secrets had to be swept firmly and deeply under the carpet. It wasn't so hard to do; worse things have happened to others.

As a family, the whole lot of us, ten kids, Dan, and Mom went to therapy. We were adults, Joan was a teenager. We were here with this therapist, a slight woman is what I recall, in a large office in Gramercy Park, made small by the sheer number of us. It was my turn to speak; we were here to speak the truth, after all. The problem at hand was that my stepbrother was suffering. We shared an apartment, and I could see that he was on a downward spiral. I loved him very much. One thing Mom and Dan did right was they knit us together as a family. I loved, love, my stepsiblings. I did research with Jenny, and we learned of an in-hospital program at Yale New Haven, and we convinced him to go. He was there for thirty days. When he came out, we went into family therapy. A bit weird at twenty-six or however old I was, but in the session, it was my turn to speak. Dan's eyes were on me so hard I could feel the grip and it hurt. He looked terrified of what I might say. Joan, his favorite, his love, his life, sat right next to him, oblivious of the secret. I was jealous of her. I felt mean. I wanted to say exactly what had happened. We were in therapy, after all. I have no recollection of what words came out of my mouth, but I know the truth was not among them. Before I had time to say much of anything, Dan blew out of his chair in a rage, terrifying the therapist, who jumped out of her seat. After that I spoke no more; there were other things to speak about now.

(Now I must add this complicating fact: Joan was not there. She was in college, unable to attend. She told me this recently when I recounted for her my memory of the therapy session. "I was not there," she said. Weird, unstable memory. I put her there because it felt like she was there, that that was why Dan blew out of his chair. He did blow out of his chair as I was about to speak. Danny recalls his father blowing out of the chair. We each remember in our own way, according to how given situations imprint on our brains, intersect with the narratives we have going on up there. Joan was not at the therapy session, but I wanted her to be part of it, the truth to be heard. The truth did come out, sideways as it likes to do, not articulated, but there all the same. I couldn't speak it; Dan spoke it through his rage. The truth of this sort hides itself despite our best efforts. Indeed, I am still trying to speak it.)

There was an earlier time when I tried to tell Joan about Dan. I wasn't a good soldier in the effort to protect Joan. Drunk at a party when she was still a teenager and my sisters and I were still in that ten-year conversation about our childhoods, Joan took us to task. She said we were negative and that she had had a beautiful childhood and that it was a character flaw to see our childhoods in a negative light. She was persistent, annoying, urgent even, like she was trying to save her own childhood without realizing it. I couldn't stand hearing her speak of that which she knew absolutely nothing about. The alcohol worked on my tongue, loosening it as alcohol likes to do and I blurted: "You'd hate your childhood, too, if your father had slept with you. Your father has slept with all of us."

That was, of course, not what had happened. In the moment, my sisters swooped in to shield Joan from me.

Time moved us away from there and it became apparent to me that, with that time, Joan had buried those words—so much so it was as if, for her, they had never been spoken. Perhaps that wasn't hard since I'd been drunk and had exaggerated, so my attempt could remain unexplored, the belly flop of a heartless sister with everything twisted up inside into a kind of nonsense. We grew up, lived a long stretch of our adult lives, but then Joan learned the truth about Dan—suddenly, shockingly. She wouldn't speak with me. She was upset with me for reasons that would take a long time for me to fully understand but that I thought had to do with the fact that I had not told her about what Dan had done, allowing her to live a lie. She lost her equilibrium. She had no idea who she was because she couldn't be the person who had been raised and adored and loved by a man who abused his stepdaughters, a mother who stood silently at his side, parents who didn't protect children—this is my interpretation. Dan was dead, twenty-five years dead.

Secrets and abuse bleed across generations, are handed down like family heirlooms—so that therapist told me, the one I did not like. The secrets have a way of seeping into the rock below, staining it.

* * *

JOAN AND I MET at the Farm. Many months had passed, maybe a year, since she had learned about Dan. I could still feel it in me, the inability to be mad at him. What was the point? One has to figure out one's own self as an adult. We can't blame. The litany of rationalizations I fed to myself. Dan was just a sad, frustrated man, now dead, very dead. I wanted to find a way to make it better for Joan, to absolve Dan for Joan. Fix it. But that is not what Joan wanted. She wanted no more lies. She wanted to make it clear that silence never remains silent. We spoke about a lot of things. She said she understood that we had all been doing our best in trying to protect her. I told her I hadn't done my best, that I had tried to tell her once when I was drunk. I told her that it had been hard for me to feel close to her, not because I didn't want to be, but because of the secret that existed between us, a thick wall that divided us and of which she had been entirely unaware. I hadn't understood why I couldn't feel as close as I would have liked. I hadn't allowed myself to explore this, shunted it away with so much else that made no sense and was too painful to explore. But here on this walk I confessed that, and it devastated her.

Every time we collected as siblings there were mythic stories of Dan. I had envied Joan her ignorance, and I couldn't bear the stories. ("Love Dan," Mom had said to us. If we loved Dan, it would validate Mom's choice. If Dan loved us, it would validate Mom's choice.)

I had a cat growing up who I loved very much. Her name was Kitty. "Here, Kitty, Kitty Kitty." It was the best I could do. After the incident in the waterbed, I took to squeezing Kitty very hard, under the pretense of love. I trapped her when she crawled inside my dollhouse. (I still played vigorously with dolls.) I gave her no way out, leaving her there until I could no longer take her meowing. I felt pain, doing this, but I still did it. I threw her across my bedroom, astonished how easily she landed on her feet, astonished by the force of my power—scared even.

Then I started stealing. I stole lots—shoplifting, my stepmother's credit card, a check from my stepmother's recently deceased mother's checkbook that I wrote out for ten bucks and cashed at the local bank. I stole a hundred-dollar bill from Dan's wallet. I felt like something was being answered, some desire to get back what had been taken from me—though I would not have been able to put it in those terms at that time or understand what it was that had been taken. Then I got caught, charged for shoplifting and stealing the credit cards, tried before a judge, threatened with juvenile detention. My stepmother pressed charges to teach me a lesson. The judge was sick of white kids from Princeton getting off for crimes that Black kids went to juvenile detention for. He, too, thought I needed to learn a lesson. The shame I still feel for this is not unlike the shame I feel about Dan.

AS DAN LAY DYING, those last painful days when he was no more than a skeleton draped in flesh lying in his bed, he summoned me. We were all there, even my grandmother who by this point had moved in with Mom and Dan, had hung the ancestors on her bedroom wall who watched over me for much of the pandemic, and kept asking from her perch in an armchair in the living room: "Is he dead yet?"

I went to Dan's bed, and I sat down beside him and stroked his thin hair.

"I hurt you," he said. "I am sorry." He said that he was sorry.

Once again, I forgave him. What was I going to say now? What were the words? What was my voice? What needed to be asked and answered? At the Abbey Pub, those years before, there was another thing he had said to me as he explained why he had done what he had done: "I was curious, Babe." Or "I was just curious." He called all of us Babe. Curious. I didn't think about that at the bedside. I thought that I didn't want him to feel bad, to die feeling remorse. I still wanted to protect him. The catarrh had already lodged in his throat, liquid bars between his parted lips.

"He said it so he wouldn't go to hell," one of my sisters later said. "He was absolving himself."

I didn't think of it that way. I thought he once again wanted me to know that it wasn't in my imagination, that it had happened, that he was wrong and bad and sorry.

"Don't glorify him," another sister said later.

What I wish I had asked and failed to even think of in the sunlit death room was about that curiosity he had had. What had he been curious about? Would he succeed in stimulating an eleven-year-old girl who had not yet, not once, tried to please herself? Had not yet, not once, felt the pleasures of sex? What experiment was he doing? Would his one violation against me reverberate across my lifetime, as his having been molested had reverberated across his? Would this abuse (a word I still find hard to say—along with the word *trauma* or *traumatized*) follow, pass on into the next generation? What was he researching that night in the waterbed? "Even if he used his fingers," a sibling said to me recently, "it's still penetration and penetration is rape."

What ever would he have answered?

What exactly were you curious about, Dan?

INSTEAD OF ALL THAT, the questions of a grown woman with a lifetime of reckoning behind her, this is what the young woman wrote about the goodbye:

11/21/94

> *I spent Saturday at the Farm and came back yesterday afternoon. Dan said goodbye to me. Essentially, he said he was sorry for having hurt me and that I had been such a good person. We cried. He told me a funny story which I asked him for. He said his mother had been spooked once coming home late in the night. She thought she heard something and turned the light on suddenly. She was standing in front of a mirror, and it caught her reflection and she jumped. "It's only you, you old fool," she said. Dan thought this was funny because it was the one moment in her entire life when she'd been able to recognize her own foolishness. This self-centered woman having some perspective on herself, enough to love to tell the story so others could laugh*

at her. Dan said he thought about it his entire life. He told me to write, write, write. I said I would and that he was my subject and I hoped he didn't mind. He said he was flattered. He told me I was smart—the one thing I wanted from him all my life. I felt like he gave me a gift yesterday. He asked the Lord to protect me and love me, watch over me. I have the recollection that he said he would miss me, and he was sorry he wouldn't see what would happen to me. But I don't think he said that. I think I added that. But it felt like that's what he said. We hugged and cried and then we said goodbye. Hugging he was afraid I would crush him, yet I wanted to cling to him and hug him for comfort and to protect me as if he were my father, that kind of hug only a father can give a daughter—when you feel so warm and strong against everything outside of that hug.

The complicated illusions of love at the expense of one's self. And once again, in my own journal, I do not write what Dan had done.

AT THE FARM, JOAN and I were talking about this long-held secret. Secrets never do work out well. When I told her it had been hard for me to feel close to her, she began to cry. I hadn't explained myself well. It wasn't her but the secret. I couldn't excavate the layers and depths of what I meant. I didn't have the words. In ways I wouldn't have consciously been able to explain, I had seen her as the unspoken exception, the untouched, unsullied experiment internalized by the family. The jealousy. Why should she be free when we weren't? Why should she be protected when I hadn't been? For years, part of me rebelled against this. It was all unconscious and avoidant, but even so, whatever it was, it created a barrier. Then the meteorite hit her life, making indelible what was already clear but camouflaged like so much else: Joan was not the exception. She had not escaped. She was just the last to know.

In not feeling close to Joan, I lost out—another casualty, another loss to acknowledge, understand, and fight to reclaim. To see her, to see myself.

We walked down the long driveway; we walked across the field; we walked to the pool and sat on a couch watching the evening come on and tree frogs dive into the water. The sky spilled color. When she was little, she would say that when she grew up, she would do whatever it took to have ten children and she would raise them at the Farm. She lived in Los Angeles and had no intention of returning here.

"Have you ever written about this?" she asked. I knew that she had not read my early novels; I had imagined she was afraid of what she might find in them.

"I've never written about this. We were taught to protect you."

"You shouldn't have."

"I know. I am sorry."

"Will you write about it now?"

"I don't know," I said.

"You should," she said.

Part Two

I hadn't intended to write about Dan when I started this book. Rather, I had wanted to write about trees, my mother's forest, how I discovered it as an adult, returned home again by extraordinary circumstance. I had wanted to write about the bamboo removal, how that led me to the forest, to see that it was threatened, that it needed to be cared for, that it was a job I wanted to do. The book I had intended to write was to have been about the long but meaningful work of trying to heal a forest, in particular by tending to the forest's understory. I wanted to write about growing trees in our paddock, maple trees to be transplanted into the forest once they had grown above deer-grazing height. Our forester had all but dared me with the task, telling me that all his clients who had tried had failed: they failed because they forgot to water the trees, because as protected as the trees were (in gardens, near houses) deer got to them anyway. I had wanted to write about creating and nurturing an understory.

IN LATE APRIL OF the first spring of the pandemic, before the bamboo, before I had finished teaching for the year, my stepmother called me. Her tone was urgent. She wanted to come see me.

"Is everything okay?" I asked.

"Yes, yes," she said. She and my father still live on Drake's Corner Road in the house my father built with my mother. I came home from the hospital newborn to this house. They planted a pink dogwood to celebrate my birth. When my mother, sisters, and I moved to the Farm and Yolanda and her kids moved in, she cut down the dogwood. For years, I took that as a metaphor and held it, among a growing list of grievances, against her. It took many years for me to let go of such grievances, to appreciate Yolanda, to understand that it was too easy to see her as the wicked stepmother—as tempting as it was, the swirl of righteous indignation it could inspire. Like most children, I had been steeped in an entire genre of children's literature, bedtime stories (the ones that come after the lullabies about dying babies) written in a distant time, when lower life expectancies and the risks at childbirth carried off mothers at higher rates. By one estimate, in mid-eighteenth-century France, the chance that a woman would reach her twenty-fifth year was just 30 percent. There were plenty of stepmothers to go around, in other words, and, justly or not, in stories handed down by generations and told to children like myself at the vulnerable, magic hour of bedtime, stepmothers became recognizable villains. They heaped their divided loyalties, their casual cruelties, their meanness, their wickedness, upon young female orphaned protagonists with whom I felt a powerful emotional kinship, a righteous bond of victimhood. Yolanda had never been cruel or mean or wicked—emotions having no expiration date—but I suppose even until recently she could fill that role, unfairly, somewhere in my heart.

"I'm about to teach," I said. "I start in an hour." But she insisted. She was nearby. She arrived shortly after the call, came into the living room, and sat down with me on the couch. This was dangerous. We were in lockdown. We sat six feet apart, masked. I left the doors open. My children were in their rooms, Zooming to school. Mark was preparing his classes in our room. When he finished teaching, it would be my turn and we would switch places. I was eager, curious to know what so urgently brought Yolanda here. My mother was in the dining room, coloring at her spot, Dayana at her side, working on her business. My mother could sit there for hours, coloring in an adult coloring book, perfectly tracing within the lines. She was so proud of her work and liked to show it off. Occasionally, she could become distracted by a car parked in the driveway. Sometimes, if we weren't watching carefully, she'd disappear fast, climbing into one of the cars belonging to a tenant. More than once, we'd been summoned by the owner of the car to let us know Mom was there. She was patiently waiting, hoping to go home.

I could see only Yolanda's eyes. They looked stricken as she watched my mother. "I want to give you money," she said. "A little extra for your birthdays, to you and your sisters. I want you to use it for your mother. But please don't tell your father. I don't want him to know."

This wasn't a simple matter. It wasn't a huge sum, but the sum didn't matter.

She praised me for taking care of Mom, for food shopping for them. She told me that I was so good. I'd been doing this at this point for only five or six weeks. But I confess, I liked being praised. I liked being thought of as a hero.

She said I should use the extra money in a way that would help keep this enterprise for Mom going a little better. My sisters and I each contributed money to pay for Mom's care, but the expenses of the house were an entirely different burden. The finances of keeping Mom at home were intricate, but a memory care facility wasn't affordable and now, with the pandemic, the news of what was happening all over the country in those homes gave my sisters and me chills. It didn't escape Yolanda, or my sisters, that my being here at the Farm allowed Dayana breaks, days off, assistance—made keeping Mom here possible. But I wasn't a hero.

Yolanda had become quite concerned with her own memory. Bit by bit she, too, was losing hold. She handed me a check. On the memo line she had written "Girls Birthdays."

My father and Yolanda had fallen in love while my father was married to my mother and Yolanda was married to her husband. It had taken a long time for my sisters and me to stop characterizing her as the evil stepmother plotting to ruin our lives. We were young, dramatic, hadn't lived yet. The archetype fit into a tidy little square in our minds. She had stolen our mother's place, ruined our family, her kids had taken our bedrooms.

But life passes. You grow up. You start to see with greater nuance as you, yourself, face difficult choices. My father and stepmother were suited for each other in a way my parents hadn't been—even if I could romanticize their marriage. Mom and Dad were married twelve years; Dad and Yolanda have been married more than fifty years.

"I can't take the check," I said.

"Yes, you can," she said. "It's my money." One thing I didn't doubt was that Yolanda loved me. We sat there for a moment, the check between us. A lot was going on in my head, that I should tell my father even though she pleaded with me not to, that I would definitely call Sarah the moment Yolanda left, even if it meant I'd be late signing in for my Zoom class. I thought of all the projects the money could help with. "Martha," Yolanda finally said, "I don't want to go to a home. I think I will die before your father, but if I don't, I do not want to go to a home."

There's no guidebook for a moment like this. And if there were, under what chapter, what subheading of circumstance, under what convention of conversation would you ever find it? I reassured her. I could see why she was stricken, could feel the fear coming from her as she caught my mother with her eye. This wasn't a transaction; she wasn't buying my future help. But she was seeking reassurance as she felt her mind slipping from her. Tears pricked through my eyes. I wanted to hug her, hold her, but I couldn't. I promised her she would never go to a home.

A year later she would not remember this exchange.

* * *

AFTER SHE LEFT, I called Sarah, and we chatted in the way sisters can about family matters—part gossip, part love—on a subject that we used to weave us closer together. We decided we wouldn't cash the check, but we wouldn't destroy it either. In June, Yolanda asked me about the check, asked me to please cash it. Uncashed it was messing up her accounting. Then the bamboo and septic fiasco occurred, and the amount was enough for a deposit. I did as Yolanda asked. The amount was only a fraction of the cost, but it was a start; it helped us believe we could find the rest of the needed money and finding the rest of the money would lead me out of the bamboo.

I had a concrete problem to solve, and I can be good at this. Sarah and I continued searching for other means. We could sell firewood. We could sell objects from around the house, some of the Haitian art, I thought. "If you sell any of the Haitian art, I will never speak to you again," Sarah said. Sarah had the historian's penchant for saving and preserving. Mark and I scoured the internet for what the new cannabis laws would be come November, how much it would cost to get a business off the ground. We dreamed up names: Omega Farms, Omega Grown, Rocktown Works. We could take a table at the local flea market.

But all these schemes had long-term horizons. I needed cash now.

This wasn't all that we were doing. We were taking care of my mother; we were preparing meals for the family; we were baking bread; we were food shopping for my father and stepmother; we were teaching our classes; I was publishing the novel, giving the

Zoom readings; there were chickens to be fed and nursed back to health when they got sick—and they got sick, a bloody intestinal thing that killed two; there was our son, a sporty, social sixteen-year-old for whom all sports and most social interaction had ceased; there were bills; there was our colossal debt; there were problems looming everywhere one looked—not the least of which was the growing sense of broken politics, broken government, mob-fueled unreason, all my ancestors watching in disbelief from the walls, as afternoons, mornings, evenings, in the context of what looked like the beginning of a wholesale societal collapse, it seemed I did the most absurd of things: talk about the novel I had written. There was this one, abiding, and singular fact, a gnawing feeling in the gut, that none of this would ever be enough. It's true we had each other, my husband and I, but the other thing we had, it seems, was a shared sense that none of all the things we did would ever be enough.

And yet, something else emerged, too. The scoundrels of history could make off with their loot, the scoundrels of finance could do the same, the world could sink into that swamp, but I would stay upon this hill that wasn't mine. I would make it right. I would fix it. I would make it work. There had to be a way.

I went down into the basement and looked at all the negatives—hundreds of thousands of negatives in huge, three-ring binders in boxes, shelved on every wall. Color and black-and-white, two and a quarter film, sharp, artfully shot, rare. The way they say that some musicians have an ineffable, unteachable trait called "feeling," such that even a wrong note sounds great, my mother had "feeling" when she was behind a camera. There was genius in her work. She had the ability to capture people in their most candid and beautiful moments at the happiest times of their lives. She could make babies who weren't yet smiling smile, turn a pimply and sulking teenager into happiness. But there was also complexity, depth beneath the veneer, a real person. She could see what others missed, and with that vision she captured what people wanted, for the rest of their lives. Pryde Brown Photographs, owned and operated by my mother, had been the go-to photographer for Princeton. There was barely a home in town that didn't have her portraits hanging on the walls. If selling Mom's negatives to raise money for the pool had taught me anything, it was that people wanted those negatives. My initial efforts had been with the low-hanging fruit, those customers who had been easiest to find. The further from the present, the harder it became to find the people. But Mom had saved everything. Along with the negatives, she also saved the invoices and her datebooks.

I realized I was sitting on a legacy that glimmered, faintly, of John Ringo's gold. I started working through the files, gathering phone numbers, and, through trial and error, developed a system of prospecting, with Atlanta, Georgia, as a crucial processing hub. My sister Sarah, architectural historian, could track down the provenance of documents owned by somebody's brother's second cousin during the quattrocento like nobody's business. She was the sister who, at nine years of age, could find our phone numbers when Mab Goldman, thirty-nine years old, tried to keep them from us. Soon Sarah applied these formidable research skills to tracing the working phone numbers of people whose lives had more recently been blown about and scattered. Sarah would find a working number, I would make the call, and often the pitch I'd make—of family history preserved in portraiture, of people at their best—would prevail, and we would make a sale.

Bar mitzvahs, bat mitzvahs, christenings, newborns, family portraits, fiftieth anniversaries, engagements, and weddings weddings weddings. There were hundreds of banker's boxes filled with negatives; hundreds of alphabetized binders ordered by year lined the bookcases. Inside were so many lives. The search often led to dead ends: these happy moments, frozen in time, hadn't always ended so well. There was death. There was divorce. There was a famous starlet from a famous television show in the 1990s who shortly after her wedding killed a woman while driving drunk. She ended up in prison. There was a husband tried for child molestation in a DC court. There were all sorts of fascinating careers—musicians, horse trainers, organic gardeners, shrinks, a cannabis retailer, a belly dancer. And there were moments that seemed made for a novel that I had yet to write: a divorced husband, for instance, who, after I'd given my pitch, after we'd shared some fond memories of my mother and her photography studio, and after the momentum of our conversation began to luff its sails, wondered, quietly, hesitantly, if I'd spoken to his ex-wife, wondered if I knew anything—anything at all; it didn't have to be specific—about her, about where in the world she lived, how or what in the world she might be doing with herself. He was as in the dark about her as anybody could be about someone with whom he was still clearly in love.

We tracked down prospects in a widening circumference—in Princeton and Rocky Hill and Pennington, but also in Utah, Colorado, California, England, Scotland, Switzerland, France, China. A few had awful things to say about Mom, promises she'd failed to deliver on, but mostly they were overjoyed, loved Mom. "She was special." "She was a treasure." "Oh, how she made our wedding the best." She solved problems, offered opinions and advice. "I was twenty-five when I got engaged," one woman told me. Mom instructed her that twenty-five was too young for marriage. "I waited until I turned twenty-six," the woman said. To another woman Mom told her to keep her own last name. "Don't give up your name," Mom had warned. That customer didn't.

Several people came to the Farm to collect their negatives in the summer lull of the pandemic, brought the photos of their children Mom had taken to show her, sat with her at the picnic table outside on the deck and told her stories about what had become of the kids. One woman made it a regular part of her weekly routine until the world shut down again, coming the long distance from her home to stop in and chat with Mom. Overwhelmingly, Mom's customers loved her and cared and were delighted to receive the unexpected call from me.

I would look around the basement, at the negatives everywhere, and couldn't help but reflect on how hard my mother had worked. There were quite literally hundreds of thousands of negatives. Forty years of negatives. Forty years of Mom behind the camera, looking up at her subjects, directing them to relax their lips, to think about something funny, asking them about their loves, their children, their parents, their jobs, schools, lives. She cared.

If I'd been something other than a novelist—a business tycoon, say—I might have seen that selling old wedding negatives from my mother's basement involved what tycoons call a *low rate of return.* Spending hours on the phone talking to my mothers' former customers brought a wealth of stories for a fiction writer, but for the broken homestead I had taken on, the flood that needed fixing, the income flow we made from selling the negatives, though steady, was also painstakingly slow.

BEFORE ANTHONY THREW IN the towel and told me to cover the sprouting bamboo with industrial black plastic (which, by the way, I seriously considered until I learned the cost, $2,000, and thought about how I'd dispose of all the plastic when finished with it, the environmental crime of all that plastic—not to mention the fact that his idea of smothering the new bamboo shoots might not work), he told me that I should consider harvesting trees in the forest. He told me there was value there, pointing to the forest behind the house.

"You've got a lot of trees in there," he said that afternoon. I was confused, consumed with worry. He pointed again to the forest. "Virgin trees, straight as arrows," he said. "You've got a lot of ash."

The ash were being eaten alive by the emerald ash borer. "Get them while you can," Anthony said.

Anthony had been climbing trees since childhood and had turned that early passion into a profession. He had an arborist's knowledge and love of trees but his bread and butter was residential removal—to identify potential risks that trees could pose to homeowners, to climb those trees and cut them down. In his years of climbing and cutting, he'd made acquaintance with a trade and subindustry whose presence I had not suspected could exist in the country's most densely populated state: lumberjacks and logging. The lumberjacks and loggers of New Jersey were an unforeseen (at least by me) group of swashbuckling chainsaw men who knew the middlemen who paid cash over the barrelhead for trees and sold those trees to lumber mills. Anthony mentioned a few names and suggested I might give them a call.

"But be careful," he said one day before he left. "They're all pirates. They're sweet-talking and friendly, but every single one of them is a pirate. Don't forget that."

I HAD ALWAYS THOUGHT our forest was like a background setting, with animals, that mostly took care of itself. When I was a child my mother and Dan would organize expeditions down to the pond, where we'd skate and build bonfires that glowed against the dark amphitheater of trees surrounding us. The pond existed in the first place because beavers had blocked a creek and built a lodge there. If you walked along the pond's shore, you could see the small stumps of young trees with the toothmarks the beavers had made. In the summers, my stepbrothers and little sister would Daniel Boone it all day out there, fishing in the pond and shooting rifles. There was even a haunted house in the middle of the woods that Dan said was once owned by the actor Claude Rains, the villain in *Casablanca* and countless other films from that era. Even the canopy of trees by our house offered a kind of history; the breeze blowing through them seemed to whisper it.

In the very early spring, shortly after we'd arrived, Livia and Jasper would return from their long hikes glowing with enthusiasm. "It's enchanted," they said. They insisted on showing us and we marveled, the trees bare and still dormant. The trails were neatly maintained by the land trust. Stone steps; tree-trunk bridges over a swollen creek; tidy, well-groomed trails rolled on for miles. Deep in the woods we were alone, and it was silent, spooky, magical. But the trees were still just trees for me, a collective, some taller, some shorter. As a child my father had taught me to identify trees: "Strike one, strike two, strike three, you're out. Pitch pine," he'd say, explaining how to both identify pitch pine (the needles are in fascicles of three) and also to remember. But I hadn't remembered much of anything. Reading Richard Powers's *The Overstory*, I related to a couple who never thought anything about trees, until suddenly they were forced to. "They're not hard to find: two people for whom trees mean almost nothing."

Now with Anthony's suggestion about the ash, with the mounting money issues, I started to notice the trees in a way I hadn't before. He took me into the woods to show me what he was talking about. It was summer and the trees were in their glory, the canopy so tight the sun struggled to get through. Looking straight up the trunk of an ash, an oak, a poplar, I began imagining what this tree had seen, right here, in this spot of the forest. A big conversation was taking place. The leaves and branches spoke of it, but to hear it would require something more than I possessed.

Soon I could identify an ash, a poplar, an oak, beech, birch, cedar, dogwood, maple. There were well over a hundred ash in our forest, more than a few of them "balding," I could see, the bark stripped away, laying bare the flesh of the tree. The larvae of the emerald ash borer get under the bark and eat their way around the trunk until water and nutrients can no longer flow to keep the trees alive. The trees become hollow giants easily toppled in a storm. Further, the larvae attract woodpeckers, who peck and strip away at the bark as they feed, leaving telltale scarring on the trunks. The trees all across the nation are infested and dying by the hundreds of millions and have been for some twenty years since the EAB, as it is called, first appeared, traveling from Asia on the backs of freight packaging.

With Anthony, looking up at all the ash, an entire grove of ash, ash everywhere, as far as I could see, beautiful, white ash, skyscraper tall, I realized that the forest was a more complicated organism than I'd allowed—even this small forest of my mother's—but the idea of cutting down a tree, even a dying tree, repelled me. "Some people don't like to cut trees down. I get it. But these, they're dead men walking," Anthony said. "Get the money." Then he gave me a brief lesson in what makes for good lumber, showing me with gestures how tall, straight, and unmarred the butts of the ash were. Though so many of our ash were still healthy, still free of the borer, it was shady business trading in them—I would come to understand later. Ash, historically, was a productive wood, good for furniture, flooring, doors, cabinetry molding, hockey sticks, oars, baseball bats. Ash had been the preeminent wood of bats, bats made of ash were used by Joe DiMaggio, Roger Maris, Babe Ruth, Ty Cobb, to name just a few. In the early 2000s, the maker of the Louisville Slugger, Hillerich & Bradsby, was making 800,000 ash bats per year, most of them for major leaguers. Not anymore. A whole nation of ash, an entire globe of ash is dying, as the elms had when I was a child and the chestnuts before that.

Where branches start to shoot out from the trunk, the board value stops, and firewood begins. Some of the butts, unmarred, were as long as thirty feet. "Veneer quality in there, I'm guessing," Anthony added. Then he told me again to watch out for the pirates.

Returning to the yard, he pointed to all the ash looming tall above the main house. I saw them in a new way, dead men walking. There were so many of them. All of them were dying or would die, some right above the house. "Two years max," Anthony said. You could already see the balding on some; a couple were just enormous sticks. "If you're smart," Anthony said, "get your pirate to start with those. Hiring me or some other company will cost a few thousand a tree. Get the logger to take them as part of the deal."

AS IT HAPPENED, WE had a forestry plan and had had one for many years—a Woodland Management Plan and Forest Stewardship

Plan. Our forester's name was Duke. Years and years before, I accompanied my mother to Duke's office, which was nearby in Rosemont. We were there to pay some fee or other. I remembered him as a handsome, older man with a bit of an outdoor swagger. The Woodland and Forest plan was a document with instructions for managing the land. Duke redrafted it every ten years and then oversaw its execution annually. Having the plan allowed Mom a tax deduction from the state, but it required that she keep vines off the trees, turn downed trees into firewood to be sold, that she harvest a crop (hay) in our field, that she show some income from the venture.

To confirm Anthony's ash prognosis and to find out more about the prospect of harvesting them, I called Duke. "They're all dead even if they aren't dead yet," he confirmed of the ash. "They are dead," he repeated. I asked if there was anything we could do to save them. He laughed, told me we had over a hundred, that the medicine would be expensive and would only delay the inevitable. "Nothing to do," he then said. He had a gruff, pessimist's way of speaking. (Or was it a realist's way of speaking?) He offered to come over and show me some things about the forest.

I imagined he'd be quite old, as I awaited his arrival some days later. But he wasn't old or didn't appear old. Rather he seemed younger than I was, like he'd gotten younger, still with his tough-guy swagger. I was prepared for a hike in the woods, boots, gloves. He told me we didn't need to bother going into the woods; he could show me what he wanted to show me simply by walking to the edge of a specific stand. It was behind a small red barn where we had kept our chickens when I was a girl. Far enough away from the house that it had scared me as a kid to feed the chickens at night. Knowing that, Dan had once hidden out there, jumping from behind the barn to scare me and my stepbrother Tony. Dan had draped himself in a white sheet. There was all sorts of scaring of each other as kids. All of Dan's children were experts in it. His daughter Carrie once told me that we had to worry about the Hells Angels, that they would come for us in a pack on their Harleys, that it was something they did, took women, raped them, cut off their breasts and fried them up like eggs.

When we first moved to the Farm and bedrooms were created for the McPhee girls, mine was in the basement, a finished basement with a playroom. My mother fixed the bedroom up with a carpet, a four-poster bed, curtains that matched the bed's coverlet. I had my own bathroom. But there were three holes in the wall and the holes scared me. I asked why there were holes in the walls. "It's an old house," Dan had said. "Ghosts live in there. The holes are how they get in and out." He smiled at me, that flirtatious, half-cocked smile. The holes terrified me. My mother concealed them with pieces of wood shaped like rabbits, painted white with pink ears. Even so, I refused to sleep down there. Instead, I rented it out to a friend of my stepbrother's so he could take his girl there, charging him $15 an hour. I never slept in that bedroom. Instead, I slept with Sarah at the foot of her bed, curled up like a dog.

* * *

DUKE AND I STOOD near the red barn, and he pointed to the forest behind it, drawing my attention to tall trees in the distance. In between us and the taller trees there were no small trees, no big trees, no trees at all in a space roughly two acres in size. The trees that had been there came down during Sandy, the hurricane that devastated the region in 2012. The treeless "Sandy Stand," as Duke referred to it, was thick with brambles, brambles with thistles and thorns, impenetrable. "Your forest is dying," he said.

"What?" I asked in disbelief. He wasn't a naturally friendly man. He looked at me and said simply, "There's no understory and no opportunity for an understory. The deer and those thickets make it impossible for saplings to survive." He told me he was retiring. He was done with forestry. It was headed on a path to nowhere and much devastation.

"Not a good time to be a forester," he added.

I had never given much thought to my mother's forest or to forests in general. I knew we needed forests but faced with this news I was suddenly paying attention. "There must be something that can be done," I said.

"Nothing," he said.

"I don't believe that," I said.

Finally, he smiled. "Are you rich?"

I laughed.

"You'd need to be extremely rich to do something about this forest."

I heard him, but I didn't believe him. Something stirred in me.

We walked back to his truck. I wanted him to get in his truck and drive away. I wanted an optimist. As he was leaving, and almost as an aside, I asked him about the ash, if he thought I could sell them, if he knew a logger I could call. He laughed some more, more heartily, and told me it was too late for that. "The ash are finished. No value there."

I couldn't help myself: "Don't you have any good news?"

"There's no good news here. Sorry." Then he was off, driving down the long driveway.

I called Anthony to ask his opinion.

"He's an old curmudgeon," Anthony said. He knew Duke through the tree business.

"He looks younger than when I last saw him, years ago. He doesn't age."

"He must have a girlfriend," Anthony said.

Before signing off, he gave me some names and numbers of loggers to call.

I WASN'T TRYING TO solve my childhood—or at least I didn't consciously think so. That isn't possible, and what would solving it even mean? I fell down this rabbit hole when the pandemic brought me home again. I had no deliberate quest. The past emerged from proximity to memories of it. But I was definitely continuing the conversation with the Farm, with Dan, with the Dan who had a vision for this place: the Omega Point. His library; his stand of forsythia lining the driveway; his orchard of apple, cherry, and peach trees; his bamboo forest that had been planted in part for those peacocks of his who like to feed on bamboo; his indoor swimming pool; his barn built by the stranger, Serge, who stayed ten years, the stranger who became something of a best friend for Dan, who when Dan was dying became the caretaker of Dan's secrets—letters and computer files. Serge destroyed them at Dan's request, us kids taking bets on what the secrets would have revealed.

In the 1970s, during the oil embargo, we even had a gas pump installed so we wouldn't need to wait in the long lines. We didn't have oil for the furnace, we couldn't afford to fix the broken furnace, but we had a gas pump.

Perhaps what I was doing was reclaiming, taking back control of a past that had left me powerless, trying to order and smooth it out—iron it wrinkle-free. When I dreamed about the possibilities for the Farm, owning it alone, without my sisters, wasn't the goal. My kids liked to say that it would never be mine even if it was mine, even if I owned it all. But it wasn't about owning it, having it be mine. Quite simply, I couldn't afford it anymore. Our debt had swollen since I had tried to buy it and the cost of maintaining it was prohibitive, I could clearly see that by living here. It was about something more, something that I didn't easily understand or have an easy explanation for, something ineffable. Sure, I asked myself the same questions all the time: Why was I paying so much money I didn't have to fix up a place that wasn't mine, was this just a pandemic refuge, a way of helping out my mother (and Dayana); was it the fantasy of giving my children all that I hadn't had as a child—a best version of this place?

Was I doing this for my children? Was I hoping for something out of this, some kind of recognition from my sisters that I had done so much, given so much, so they'd be grateful and proud of me, see me in my best light, as my best self? Was I doing this to be good because I wanted to be good? Was I doing this to be seen, heard? Was I doing this to feel finally worthy—beautiful and smart? That I am enough? This all dwelled in my imagination, swirled there the way stuff that doesn't make sense can. It was all of this and none of this.

My children were almost grown-ups and about to leave our six-month lockdown. Livia was heading back to college until Thanksgiving. Come mid-September, Jasper's high school would be in person every other week. Across the fall he'd be in New Jersey a week on, a week off. Whatever my fantasy was, I was here; I was deep into here—and right now we had a septic problem that needed fixing, rhizomes and root balls that needed to be removed, and all of this needed to be paid for. So, I had my eyes on the ash trees.

I also had my eyes on the chickens and the garden. In July, a full-grown hen, an Ameraucana, white feathers flecked with black, puffy cheeks and furry feet, laid the first blue egg. Finding it was like finding a miracle. I'd planted dahlias around the exterior of the garden, and they were bursting forth. The onions and shallots I planted when we first arrived were ready to be harvested, dried, and braided. The white rose flourished. The climbing yellow roses I'd planted near a trellis to hide the pool equipment were doing what they were meant to do. I had geraniums in pots, a splash of red against the day. Cucumbers and beets and a bounty of kale, zucchini, and herbs thrived in the garden—so much we couldn't eat it all. Baby lettuce and carrots, string beans, eggplant, peppers. The fig tree had produced one succulent fig that first year, which I had eaten straight off the tree. I had never done this before, and I liked it; I was curious; I was good at it. Somewhere in here was my reckoning with the past.

There was a blight on the forest and upon the body politic—people were still dying needlessly by the thousands daily, the living paralyzed by the obscene spectacle of unreason, yet the garden surprised us with its bounty: overnight, it seemed, zucchini emerged as big as a dog; fist-sized tomatoes, turning from green to red, released their grip with the slightest tug on the stem; the bladed leaves of Swiss chard sprang from their beds as big as fans on a pharaoh's pleasure barge; a soft breeze carried the scent of peppery arugula and sweet basil; the rooster offered his intermittent and reassuring commentary that life would spill forth, even here in the rocky Sourlands.

ON SUMMER EVENINGS I would take Mom to the garden. "Beautiful," my mother would say, walking with me at sunset. "The light," she'd say. "Look, there," she'd say. "Look at the sky. Do you see it?" I would agree, and then I would indulge myself a little.

"Look at the trees, and the house," I'd say. "Isn't it all so beautiful here?"

"Oh, it is. Beautiful."

"Do you know who owns this house?" I'd ask.

She'd look at me as if I'd asked her to quote a theorem from Anaxagoras.

"No. Who?"

"You do, Mommy."

"Me? Really?"

"I'm not kidding, Mommy."

And each day she forgot—each day she won the lottery, and each day I got to hand her the winning ticket. Was that what I was doing this for?

Sometimes on evening walks with my mother, I'd feel an urgency creep into me, a desire to fix the place while she was still alive, so she could see it as it had never been, to bring it to its full majesty. When she was fifty-nine, after my stepfather had died, she surprised us all: she fell in love again to a man she'd known since she was nineteen. They'd had a frisson, a special bond across both her marriages. It was as if their love had been spectacularly misplaced across an ocean, an entire lifetime, until it suddenly wasn't—until the day she could tell me that, at fifty-nine, her life was just beginning.

She'd put everything she'd had into this place, and now, as she, the person behind those eyes, slowly disappeared from view, the place replaced her, as places do. A sign fashioned by the Delaware & Raritan Greenway at the bottom of the gravel driveway said so. For all who cared to drive here, walk up the road, hike on the trails in this forest, the place would, ever after, bear her name: Pryde's Point. Not the Omega Point, rather Pryde's Point.

Then always she asked, "And who are you? Do I know you?"

* * *

IN THE LATE 1990S, my mother sold the rights to develop her land to the D&R Greenway. My stepfather had died a few years earlier. He had not been my stepfather, legally, until a few months before he died. His marriage to my mother in Haiti wasn't recognized by the state of New Jersey. As a result, my mother had no definite rights to the Farm. Legally it was Dan's, and the loose way that Mom and Dan had done things during their life together didn't protect my mother, even though she had put everything she made into the Farm. The only urgent thing Dan wanted to do before he died (apart from having Serge destroy his secret files) was marry Mom so the deed would transfer upon his death immediately to her. He managed to accomplish that.

One of the first things she did as her own act at the Farm was to put it into the land trust. It remained hers and she could do as she pleased with it except subdivide or build new structures or extend the footprint of existing structures. In exchange for selling the rights to develop, Mom was given a sum of money that allowed her to renovate the house, to make it her own as well. She ripped out the 1960s orange laminate kitchen, closed off inconvenient doors, opened up others, expanded windows to allow in more of the view, redid a bathroom. Gone was the tight, closed-in kitchen of my childhood. Though it wasn't a huge overhaul, it was a signature. The house was Mom's now.

These were heady years for my mother. All I had to do to be reminded of this was look at her appointment books, neatly saved for just this purpose, I supposed, downstream. The days are so filled with photo shoots and sittings and weddings, but there are also the mammograms, the dentist, all the visits from her daughters or to her daughters. *Sarah comes; Joan's goodbye party; Martha's birthday; Laura to India; Jenny here from Italy.* And then there was Nick. *Nick here* with a red line drawn through a good many days. The days empty for Nick. Nick was a roommate of my father's on his postcollege year at Cambridge to study English literature. Nick was married already with a baby on the way, but it didn't stop him and Mom from falling in love at first sight when he came to pick Mom up at the train station as a favor for my father. My mother had been in France on her junior year abroad and had taken the train and the boat and then the train again to see my father in England.

Nick was born on a tobacco farm in what was then Rhodesia, now Zimbabwe. A thinner version of Sean Connery, he'd married an heir of some sort who had thousands of acres and a castle spreading out along the Firth of Clyde in Scotland. When I was growing up, Nick was always present in our lives—visiting us when my parents took us to the island of Colonsay from where the McPhees descend, inviting us to visit after my father left my mother, welcoming any one of the ten of us to Skipness, their Scotland home, coming to Mom after Dan died, which is when they fell in love all over again.

Nick visiting. Looking at the blank days, the red line indicating that no appointments should interfere—I can feel and know and see, those years were hers to do with as she pleased. And she was pleased to see Nick, with nothing disturbing the days. It didn't matter to her or to him that he was still married, that he lived with his wife; there were plenty of ways for them to rationalize—Nick and his wife, *they were estranged*, or *their marriage was over long ago*, or *he's been having affairs for years.* Mom worked extremely hard; the blank days were reserved for Nick. And she loved and was loved.

He still calls her almost every day. He still sends her favorite fudge every month. Even after I moved back to New York, after my year at the Farm came to an end, by which time my mother had forgotten who he was and could no longer formulate much of a sentence, she always managed to ask him, "When are you coming? I want you to come."

IT'S NO MYSTERY THAT the mother-daughter relationship is the most complex relationship to exist. When I was a little girl, I never wanted to leave my mother. That's how it works. The child's job is to separate, the mother's job is to help forever. "It's all the mother's fault," I liked to say, both in moments of jest and of fury.

When my daughter was seventeen, she separated with such violence, I came apart, went into a depression that seemed to last a long time. I refused to see my friends and my sisters. Livia's anger involved my family history and she wanted nothing to do with them. This endured through her freshman year of college and then it started to wane. She'd found herself and her confidence, and the tide that was the teenage years receded, leaving a beautiful, centered woman. Then the pandemic came, and she was returned to me, this magnificent person who made each day a good one to be living through. She too felt the weird blessing, that we got something back as all around us the world crumbled, the cataclysmic realities brought on by a virus. Everyone, it seemed, was keeping gratitude lists—she was mine.

In 2012, when my mother's dementia first became evident and Sarah closed down her business, my mother started spending a lot more time with us in New York. At first it was a few days per month, a week, two weeks. The time with us increased as the dementia progressed. Our apartment is a two-bedroom, but we had made a makeshift room for my son in the dining room and my mother slept in there with him in his bed. He was eight when this began, and he loved sleeping in bed with his grandmother. She could still tell stories; she was still to him who she had always been—indulgent, spoiling, funny, loving beyond measure. The shared room went on for years, until he went to boarding school and my daughter to college.

This arrangement of Mom's extended stays with us began in part because of proximity. I didn't have the money to contribute to her care initially as my sisters had, so I contributed my time. My mother hadn't been good financially, didn't have retirement accounts. Having my mother with us in New York saved on paying the part-time caregiver we had in New Jersey. If Mom was with me, that expense was alleviated. I also lived closest to her. At this point, all my sisters lived much farther away—Los Angeles, Boston, London, Atlanta. But there was more to it, as there always is. I felt I was getting my mother back, entirely to myself, like when I was a little girl and my sisters were ferried off to school on the yellow school bus, leaving Mom and me alone with the long day before us to be together.

But things got weird. Mom, who always loved to make things beautiful, to make arrangements of fruit, of flowers, of silver on a shelf—her moments, I liked to call them—started making strange arrangements, with a discarded banana peel, say, and used Q-tips, rotten strawberries. On several occasions, she left the apartment in the night while Mark and I slept, returned to us by the doorman. On other occasions, she eluded the doormen and we had to hunt her down, terrified we'd lost her. Once I found her deep in the night in the stairwell several floors below my apartment, in her underwear, crying.

Her New York visits and my caregiving ended abruptly. I couldn't do it anymore. Jasper suffered two concussions (one from football on the first day of classes, the second at the start of the second term—the result of a flagrant foul in basketball) and needed to take a medical leave from boarding school. To keep him in his grade, I decided to homeschool him. I called Sarah and she flew in from Atlanta. We put our minds together, called everyone we knew, spread the word. Within a day we hired a full-time caregiver, and I found the money for my portion of the contributions by going into debt.

IN MARCH 2020, WHEN the pandemic struck, my decision to return to New Jersey was immediate. I wanted to be with my mother. The world was closing down. The massive ship of state, *America, Incorporated*, was sailing into uncharted waters that seemed to combine scenes from *The Manchurian Candidate* with every zombie movie ever made. Indeed, the game our family used to play on long highway trips—Zombie Apocalypse!—now flashed before us in living Technicolor. Other things flashed before us, too: the sense that all of us living in a twenty-first-century age of terabytes and algorithms and Large Hadron Colliders had been struck down by a plague without a cure. The best all of us across the globe could do, in response to this blunt fact, harkened back to medieval forms of self-isolation, or to quaint, nineteenth-century modes of hygiene—mask-wearing and handwashing. We were thrown back into a bewilderment like the one that must have taken hold of the generation of men and women who survived the catastrophe of the First World War and the pandemic forever associated with it. Like them, we, too, were suddenly grappling with the sense that something was fundamentally wrong with the way we thought about the most basic things. Like earlier poets, painters, composers, we sought to get to the bottom of what was wrong with us, collectively—a quest for fundamental truths of the self, of the person, of the individual, and her relationship to the world.

I am here.

Why am I here?

How did I get here?

(The questions I continually was asking of myself.)

The pandemic made this need to ask unmistakably clear, but, in the fullness of time, and in other ways that flashed before us, the pandemic was also a symptom of other ills.

* * *

AS I MADE MY way in the growing heat of a New Jersey summer, sometimes wearing boots and a bikini, my pick mattock descending upon a track of bamboo rhizomes, nobody would mistake me for a philosopher or an aesthetic revolutionary, but it was impossible to miss the way one's own history could rhyme with an earlier era. Whatever was happening in the crazy world outside the Farm, I would get to do something I had longed to do even if I hadn't been able to articulate it: I could return to my mother and take care of her again, be with her again, but this time armed with a caregiver, Dayana, and my family for support. I would return home again, better equipped with understanding and experience, my own agency. The phrase "You can't go home again" means, mostly, that we change over time. Home doesn't change, but we do. The "you" is no longer the "you" of yore. Perhaps there's a god, or gods, to thank for that, or perhaps there's just this one, long backward glance, in which, each day, we come face to face with this paradox of existence: that we are what has happened to us, yet, at the same time, perhaps with an even greater sense of force, *we are also not what has happened to us.*

P art of the arrangement with D&R Greenway is that they send a land steward on a regular basis to inspect the land, make sure that the habitat is being maintained so that the preserved land can thrive and "to assure that the property will be retained forever in its natural and undisturbed condition."

The most recent land steward was a young woman named Tina with a degree in forest ecology and a deep understanding of the role of invasive species. I'd never taken a property walk with an environmentalist. I knew of these visits, had been sent the reports, had even been the contact person, along with Sarah, for the reports, questions, concerns, arrangements about visits. But I hadn't focused on it before; I hadn't lived here. But I was now, and Tina called in the late summer to schedule the visit to inspect the land. She was dressed in long pants and a long shirt made of a fabric that repelled not only insects but also thorns. She wore gloves, an orange hat (hunting season had started), and in a holster at her hip she carried a pair of clippers like a gun. She had long dark hair and a round pretty face, dark brown eyes.

I showed her what I'd done with the bamboo, discussed with her the possibilities for getting out the rhizomes and the root balls. I even demonstrated my efforts with the pick mattock. She was kind and knowledgeable, not a fan of covering the swath in industrial black plastic. She explained that most bamboo needs to be dug out, that you need to get under the root balls by a good two feet and then essentially sift out the remaining roots. "It's a big undertaking," she acknowledged.

It turned out that the annual letter from D&R Greenway in 2018 encouraged us to manage the bamboo, that it was creating problems that would only get worse. It also threatened to invade the forest, adding another unwanted species. But no one was really paying any attention so the handyman we had at the time would hack it back a little and then spray it with poison, as Sarah had instructed me to do. This approach had only seemed to encourage the bamboo to fight back harder.

Tina and I took a walk through the woods, along the well-groomed trails maintained by the D&R volunteers. At the foot of our driveway there is a kiosk with a trail map, the one with my mother's name in big bold letters, showing hikers the routes they can travel and how they connect to adjacent preserved land. People love to hike these trails. As my children had discovered, the forest is magical. Across the pandemic, with everything else closed, hikers came and came. We could see them traipse across the field with their walking sticks, sometimes losing their way and ending up in our garden. There was something welcoming about them, something hopeful. Always there was their enthusiasm for the forest.

As Tina and I made our way around the loop of the darkened woods, she taught me about the various invasive species having their way with the forest floor, the vines climbing up the trees, doing their best to choke them. Multiflora rose, Japanese barberry, Oriental bittersweet, Chinese privet, bush honeysuckle, wineberries. Indeed, the forest was thick with brambles, impossible to penetrate, as Duke had shown me in the Sandy Stand. Tina pulled out her clippers and nipped the vines now and again, offering advice on how to manage the brambles, what kind of clippers to buy, letting me know how the plants spread with a vengeance, the seeds traveling in bird droppings, on the soles of shoes, on the wind. They can burrow into the ground, staying there for years until the right conditions allow them to emerge.

She also showed me what was beautiful about the forest, the variety of native plants and trees that needed tending. We had flowering dogwood, spicebush, blackhaw viburnum, bitternut and mockernut and shagbark hickories, so many tulip poplars, white and red oak, maple. She scratched at the bark of a spice tree and invited me to smell it—warm and fragrant as a sweet spice. I liked Tina. She knew what she was talking about, but she also ignited my curiosity, made me want to learn more. She could see the forest. She wasn't just looking at green and brown, which was how I saw it, large planes of color. Her sight was accurate, precise, teased out, educated, and I wanted to see better. She was also earnest, genuine. There was nothing jaded or cynical, as there was with Duke. Listening to her, I felt like something could be done for the forest. Sure, it would be hard work, but work was all it was. I had the sudden desire to buy myself a holster and an expensive pair of sharp Swiss clippers. I was fifty-six years old. It had been a long time since a subject made me curious in the way that the forest did, the invasives as they laid siege to the native species—ecology at work, the survival of the fittest before my eyes—a problem, but with a solution.

The invasives were thriving, in large part, because of the deer, Tina explained. The top priority for the forest was to suppress the deer—a euphemism for killing them. I told her we had hunters. "Good," she said. The way she said it indicated there was more, a qualifying phrase. Good . . . but.

We'd had a series of hunters since I was a kid. They'd pay Dan, then Mom, now Sarah an annual fee of about two grand to hunt the property. They'd set up stands and feeders and during hunting season they'd be out there, depending on the regulations, with a bow and arrow, or with rifles. They'd arrive at dawn, park their trucks discreetly off to the side of the driveway, and vanish into the forest. Sometimes you'd see them in the late afternoon taking off their camo by their trucks. Mark liked to go out and visit the hunters we had now. You'd hear them talking, pointing out where they'd been, what they'd done, laughing, talking some more. In these jovial, post-hunting colloquies, Mark made a point of mentioning that he and I were from New York City, that we were liberal Democrats— even worse, that we were both professors. They were extremely knowledgeable about the woods, about the entire region's ecology, where forests were flourishing, or not, and why. Theirs was the kind of local knowledge attained from years of visiting forests in different seasons, noticing what the deer were eating, sitting quietly for hours at a time and listening. They were hard-core, tobacco-chewing, pickup-driving bow-and-rifle men who worked with their hands at good jobs that needed to be done but that few people wanted to do, and their idea of weekend fun involved an almost monkish devotion to sitting alone, in the frosty predawn darkness, and waiting for something—for the wind to change direction in a way that might favor their prospects. Every so often, the great silence that surrounded the house would be broken by a shot coming from the woods. Usually this meant nothing. The sun would set, the hunters would return to their trucks, Mark would go out and visit with them, but on an evening near the beginning of firearm hunting season in the first December of the pandemic, our hunters texted him before he had a chance to step outside, inviting him to their truck to see something. He went. (They knew that I had no interest, was terrified of guns.) In the slant light of winter, the men stood around an orange snow sled which contained a beautiful buck lying on its side, its tawny coat still sleek in shades from gray to brown at the shoulders, its nose black and moist, a four-pointer. "Five, if you count this one," one of the hunters said, pointing out a nubbin of antler just beginning to form on the rack. For days, the buck had demonstrated a wily ability to outsmart and outmaneuver every trick in the hunter's arsenal of woodsmanship—but not today. Other hunters arrived in their trucks, summoned on the grapevine. Come and see. Mark said the buck was so beautiful his hands moved involuntarily toward it— to touch the wily buck—and he made a city slicker joke that maybe the buck was "just sleeping." The hunters laughed. *Just sleeping!* The hunters didn't return for the rest of the season. There was too much action in the woods, they said—all the hikers, our dogs, our kids who returned at Thanksgiving for another two-month stretch—their schools remote again for pandemic protocol.

BACK WITH TINA ON her late-summer forest visit, she explained that our hunters weren't what we needed. They were trophy hunters. We needed a professional management hunter—a no-limit, state-sanctioned agent of deer eradication who worked in volume. People do all sorts of jobs in this world, and there are people who do this: specialists with rifles and bows who deal out large-volume death upon white-tail bucks, does, and Bambis alike, donating the meat to food banks and calling it good. It's hard to argue with the ecological science supporting the culling of the New Jersey herds. The deer had lost their natural predators, Tina explained, and in many areas had reached twenty times the normal carrying capacity of New Jersey woodlands. They ate every tree sapling in sight, denuded younger trees with their antlers, ate only the native shrubs, playing the single-most significant role in the destruction of forests in New Jersey.

In time, a more complete picture of my mother's forest and its challenges emerged. But we still needed the money to pay for the septic and Anthony's idea about harvesting the ash ("harvest" soon replaced "fell and sell" for the trees, as "suppression" and "management" replaced "kill" for the deer). I summoned the courage to tell Tina about my idea for taking out the ash. Her sweet face shadowed.

I explained myself—the need to find money to help pay for the massive bamboo project that had turned into a bigger septic project. I showed her the open sewage as we returned to her truck. She was turning the whole situation around in her mind. The ecology of trees and forests extended in ways that included the ecology of property owners suddenly strapped for cash money, the fluctuating market value of American hardwoods, and timber pirates. Had any of this been part of her grad school training?

"Dead trees, the ash," she said, thinking aloud, "offer habitats for bats, birds, and other creatures. They are their homes." This was true—logs on the forest floor, debris load, were an integral part of the ecosystem—but it didn't answer the thornier question that I faced on my mother's behalf: that landowners, like her, were part of a multi-layered ecosystem, only one of which was about biology. More proximate causes of the white-tail deer problem, which was killing the forest, involved housing and land values, which were more affordable the further you got away from Philadelphia or New York City. Not far from the Farm, housing developments I'd never noticed until my husband showed them to me had sprung up. The entire mission of the D&R Greenway was to control exurban sprawl, and it didn't take the white-tail herds long to know which areas had become green islands of relative safety. Then there was another non-biological fact that Duke, the ever-pessimistic forester, had mentioned: fixing a forest is a very expensive undertaking. My sudden septic tank emergency, and my inability to pay for it, was colliding with an ecology of wealth distribution worldwide that had made debtors of us all, so it seemed. Median wages had increased just 9 percent over the last fifty years, accounting for inflation, whereas the U.S. economy had grown nearly 300 percent. Even before the pandemic, nearly 40 percent of Americans could not afford their rent or mortgage payments. There was no state in the union where a person working full-time at a minimum-wage job could afford to rent a two-bedroom apartment. A scant few were living in forests of money trees and flying around in private jets. I had rhizome removal, a septic cave-in on my hands, and no money to spare. At some point on my walk with Tina, the ash trees began transforming into a possible way out of the mess I was in—from trees to board feet of lumber. (Hardwood lumber is typically sold by the board foot.) It could have been my imagination, but Tina seemed stricken. Felling the "dead men walking" trees would cause harm to a wide cast of characters, and there was no way around this fact. What's more, the machinery required to do the job would help both spread and bury the seeds of the invasives, injure other trees that were in the way, and create soil erosion. "We'll need to look at your forestry plan," she said, and I felt chastised.

I did this immediately, and then felt vindicated, looking at the most recent ten-year plan executed in 2015. Here is part of what I found about harvesting trees in the twenty-page document, describing both the forest as it is and what should be accomplished in a ten-year time frame:

Notwithstanding attitudes regarding the harvesting of trees,
it is noted that New Jersey was recently confronted with the

fact that the emerald ash borer has arrived, and with it the reality that this beetle will result in the loss of all of the ash. Point sample data estimate that Stand 1 has a total volume of 44,000 board feet of ash with a current value of $9,700. It is recommended that, since the outcome will be the same whether the ash is killed by the beetle or is harvested, a pre-emptive harvest of the ash should be conducted to salvage as much of its value as possible.

I HAD THE NAMES of three loggers. I called all three and made dates to show them the trees—one from Pennsylvania, the other two from New Jersey. They all looked the same: swaggering, fit, a ruddy appeal, swashbuckling chainsaw men who treated me like a girl who didn't know anything. It's fair to say I knew little about taking down giant trees. We walked the lot; they admired the trees as objects of board-foot lust. They spoke of their height, of how perfectly straight they were, that they didn't branch out until the top. By this point I had read *The Hidden Life of Trees*, had learned from author Peter Wohlleben that trees had a big conversation going on that had started long before any of us were born. Trees were social creatures, sharing information, sending secret messages about everything—insects, droughts, nutrients of carbon and nitrogen, distress. The messages are transmitted through mycorrhizal networks, the symbiosis between fungi and plants at the root level that works to protect and nurture the entire ecosystem of the forest. (I've read since that there is some debate surrounding this hypothesis, but the point remains that more is happening in the forest than a novice might at first appreciate.) I told the loggers about the bats, that they made their homes in the snags. They laughed. "Animal hotels," one of them said. "But they aren't paying any rent." They said the bats would find another place to sleep. When I expressed concern about taking down trees, even a dying tree, as I flirted with the idea of these guys taking them down, they laughed some more and explained, as if they were talking to a dimwit, that forests needed to be managed. It was in the management plan, wasn't it?

Everyone had his or her own point of view. I needed cash.

I settled on a guy named Dan because he agreed, as Anthony had advised, to take the ash in the yard. He was a friendly guy who had a handsome smile and liked to chew on sassafras because that's what root beer comes from. He liked to tell me that the Indians used it to spice and thicken their food, to drink it like tea, to use in the making of their canoes. "We aren't supposed to call them Indians anymore," he said with a smirk that was both a slightly veiled grievance and evaluative overture: Did I also think it was silly that the word *Indian* was taboo when spoken by a white person? No, I most certainly did not think it was silly. An entire history of deceit, murder, and systematized violence and theft, still playing itself out in a standoff at Standing Rock, spoke against this New Jersey lumberjack's casual racism. But heaven help me, I would make nice and pretend to ignore his overture. The fact was I needed this man, who had been cutting down trees since high school. His skill might bring me close to ten grand, nearly enough to pay for half the new septic system. He said he'd start taking the trees in December.

I DREAMED MOM WAS standing over me. She had long gray hair streaked with different silver tones, beautiful. I asked her to tell me all her mistakes so that I wouldn't make them. I wanted her to tell me now, while there was still time. She was beautiful, the hair was beautiful. I tried to braid it, but she didn't want me to. She wanted to let it flow long, around her shoulders, a shawl. I persisted. What had she learned? She simply smiled, her coy flirtatious smile, which seemed to tell me that I already knew the answer. I awoke, but the dream had already crept in. I missed my mother. Sometimes deep in the night, she would appear in my room, looming above me, startling me—an actual, bodily haunting. I'd lead her back to bed. I started to cry. Mark pulled me into him and held me. I'd been impatient with Mom. I was impatient with her, with the illness. Mom had never had long hair, not once in her life.

SUMMER ROLLED INTO FALL. Because of epic storms in the gulf, because of the pandemic, because people with wealth had been stuck at home with their portfolios swelling and nothing to spend their money on except home improvements, the excavation company installing the new septic for the cottages was not just swamped; it was deluged. The bamboo culms had been removed at the end of July. In early October, sewage still emptied into the cleared area, new culms like asparagus spears shooting toward the sunlight.

One day, the excavators arrived to dig the new septic system. They came with huge machines rolling up the driveway. They used great hydraulic buckets to lift metal sheets and spread them across the lawn so the tracks of the machinery wouldn't turn the lawn into a muddy trench. That's when I asked the contractor what it cost per day to operate the machines and if he could use the machines to dig out the root balls and the rhizomes. He estimated it would take four days and cost $2,400. I would need to sell eight more sets of negatives, but the cost of leaving the bamboo was far greater. And there would be income from the harvesting of the ash. The contractor also agreed to an interest-free installment plan.

For four days, in the driving rain, I guided the man operating the excavator so that he didn't miss a root ball or a rhizome. Eight hours per day, I marched alongside the machine and one by one the powerful metal claw plucked out the bamboo. As Anthony had discovered, there wasn't just one layer, but sometimes two, even three. I dashed inside only to teach my classes. School had begun again. Mark and I were completely remote. My daughter was back to college in person for her junior year. Mark and I took turns in our apartment in the city to be with Jasper, who was now in school, in person every other week. On the weeks when Jasper was remote, we all returned to the Farm. The week of the excavation, I was at the Farm, extremely motivated to get all that bamboo out. I followed the excavator back and forth across the former bamboo grove all day long. I followed so closely the driver of the excavator had to ask me to step away for a moment so that he could pee in the woods.

I WAS GOOD AT managing, at juggling, at taking on more. Across this year, I managed my mother's home and her health, saw to it that she had a local doctor who paid regular house calls; I promoted a novel; I mothered my children; I loved my husband; I taught my classes; I concocted ideas for making money to replace the septic; I cleared the bamboo; I felled some trees in the forest and so on and on and on. I baked many loaves of bread, cooked feasts for my family, my mother, Dayana and her son, Juanpa, who finally arrived in September just as my children left. I helped Dayana with my mother, giving her days off, which she spent with her son. They set up his bedroom in the room in the basement that had once been mine. He was not afraid of it. She took more days off to visit her mother in New York City. Taking care of my mother now included taking care of her incontinence. I never stopped. I could slip from one task to the other and no one would know from where I had just come. I was a pro at compartmentalizing. No one questioned my talents and abilities, especially not I—apart from my refrain Why Was I Doing All This?

I'd dart into the house, wet from the rains in the former bamboo forest, sprayed with dirt from the excavator, and suddenly I would become Professor McPhee, Zooming with my class. After class I'd make dinner. After dinner I'd read student stories, help my son with homework. At night I'd dream about my mother. In the morning I'd wake early, collect the eggs, feed the chickens then the dogs and the cats, shop for my father, go for a run. A good friend would call, and we'd hatch plans for a visit with her daughter, could her daughter stay for a month in the summer? Of course. Dayana would need help with something, her son would need help with something, Mom would need help with something. I was good at this—it made me feel capable and proud. I was a fixer; I got stuff done. Give me more. I can handle it. Pile it on. When my kids were very young, they buried each other in all the linen from the linen closet. One nicely folded sheet, one nicely folded pillowcase, blanket, comforter all in a giant heap, taking over the living room, four or five feet high and just as wide. The little bodies of my kids squirreled around beneath the heap of sheets, proud of what they had taken on.

THE WORK OUTSIDE PROGRESSED. The septic system pipes from the upper cottage ran downhill to a one-thousand-gallon tank. Pipes from the lower cottage joined the same tank. Beyond the tank an enormous hole some twenty feet deep was dug and filled with small stones to create a leach field, the liquid part of the sewage running through more pipes from the tank to the leach field, where it seeped through the stones to disperse into subterranean depths in the forest beyond. The work took about ten days to complete, with one day of waiting on the stones for the hole and PVC pipes—the supply backup caused by the storms in the Gulf.

The contractor, a jolly, generous man with a pot belly, a red face, and a thick New Jersey accent who volunteered for the local fire department and also as an EMT, about which he enjoyed telling gruesome stories, offered to use one of his machines, a leveler, to level the driveway. "Give the guys something to do while they wait," he said. Our driveway is long, at least a quarter mile. It was pocked with potholes we'd been filling since I was a kid—one of Dan's workday specials, all ten of us kids out there with shovels shoveling in stones that sprayed out as soon as wheels rolled over them.

The driveway has its own history. It belongs to my mother's property, with an easement in place for the house that was once owned by the Viecelis, which sits at the elbow, where the driveway bends sharply to the left if you're leaving the Farm. The horse farm at the foot of our driveway, the owner of the vast field in front of our house where Dan once grew pot so long ago, has no rights to the use of the road. But a creek, the Alexauken, where George Washington camped on his way to the Delaware according to Dan's stories, makes it impossible for the horse farm to access the field without using our driveway. Before the new owner bought the place, we charged the former owner a toll of $75 a month to help with the maintenance. She happily paid the levy. The new owner said he'd take it up with his lawyers.

This property had turned over a few times in our tenure at the Farm. When I was a kid, this field was also farmed by a neighbor who had worked the land for generations, accessing the field by using our driveway. When Dan bought the Farm, he told this farmer he would need to contribute for repairs. All those potholes. The farmer refused.

Dan denied him access to the field. The farmer took Dan to court, but the judge would not hear the case, asking the farmer pointedly why in the world he assumed it to be his right to use a driveway that wasn't his? One day a dog of ours whose name I have forgotten ran across the farmer's field, and he shot it.

Locally we had a reputation, and it wasn't always a good one. We were liberal freaks and people were paying attention. Mom and Dan registered as Republicans so they could vote for candidates in the primaries who were least likely to win in the general election. There were so many of us, something was always going on up here on our hill. Friends from school were never allowed to come play. Sometimes I would ask to speak to the mother, ask her why her daughter couldn't come over. I couldn't see our reputation; I didn't understand. Rather, things could seem kind of exciting as a child: speeding down the highway in the Cadillac, a bunch of us kids in the car, a cop pulled Dan over more than once. Dan instructed us not to look at the cop, we'd appear guilty if we did. The officer leaned through the window to ask Dan for his license and registration while us kids tried hard to act normal, not to look at the officer's face, not to laugh, though one of us was always on the verge of cracking up. Dan pulled out his wallet and flashed a badge he had in there on easy display, a badge that indicated he was an honorary member of a police force somewhere in Texas, a real, shiny, official-looking badge. The cop apologized and off we drove, cruising down the highway like we were something special.

After the *People* magazine article, another occasion arose to make us (or me, in any case) feel famous. A group of Germans came to film us for a documentary they were making. I have no idea who they were or what happened to their film, but in late 1975 they took over the dining room and the living room—set up lights and cameras and one by one they interviewed us. It was the Dan-as-house-husband angle, this New American Family of blended siblings and parents—mother who worked. At first it was exciting, like the article. We would be on TV. We would be famous. But it took forever to film all of us and I remember this: I was one of the last to be filmed, wearing tight pink Jordache jeans that I had to lie down to zip up even though I was only about ten years old. My father was here to pick up my sisters and me for his weekend (court decreed), sitting in his little white Volvo in the driveway, waiting and waiting and waiting. I could see him there, his head leaning into the steering wheel. The waiting made me anxious, that kind that takes over the body completely, possessing it. My mother wouldn't let me leave because the Germans hadn't yet filmed me. She preferred for my father to wait. I hated my mother. By the time it was my turn, I was a mess of snot and tears, sitting in a chair beneath the crew's bright lights, crying while being asked, if kindly, to tell them why I was crying. I told them that my mother wouldn't let me leave because she wanted to make my father wait (New American Family, ha), and for a long time I felt worse because I'd betrayed my mother.

We were oddballs surrounded by farms. Gestalt therapy, dolphin therapy, EST retreats, messy divorces, Dan and his pot and his late checks, all the kids and the kids' friends, the renters, the Omega Point: Omega Farm. We were freaks, yes. In the first summer of the pandemic, an old acquaintance from high school, a woman I had barely known back then but with whom I was now Facebook friends, asked if she could come visit me for a couple hours. She was older than me, my sister Jenny's year. I remembered looking up to her, admiring her—long hippie hair and a casual cast-off style that rejected the Princeton preppy look of Lacoste and Fair Isle, even though her family lived on the most expensive street in town. I admired that she seemed to want to be the freak, whereas I, the freak, wanted to be the Fair Isle girl. I wondered what had become of her, so I invited her over. For two hours she talked. She had a phrase she liked to repeat: "To make a long story long," as she told me of her children, her siblings, her affair, her divorce, her weird inheritance from a stranger that the stranger's children thought was coerced. Everyone seemed to drink too much. What messes of a life a person can make, I thought as I listened, fascinated, her stories spilling into more stories as we sat by the pool where dolphin therapy (or so I had believed) had once occurred.

"You know," she said after a while and then stopped herself short. "I shouldn't say this," she said.

"Go on," I said.

"In high school we called this place the Space Farm." She paused. There were so many parties in high school. So many of us here. Kids from Princeton driving out for the night, Dan holding forth with a joint, passing it around. When I was in third grade, he and Mom invited my teacher, Mrs. Jenkins, to come for an early dinner. I was terrified he'd light a joint.

"That doesn't offend you, does it?" the high school friend asked.

THE BAMBOO FOREST WAS cleared of culms, root balls, and rhizomes, a mountain of debris that took two fifty-yard dumpsters to clear, or almost clear. One small mound of bamboo wreckage couldn't fit in the last dumpster so was left behind. I had the contractor push it to the side. He used the machine he employed on the driveway to scrape the ground of what was once the bamboo forest. Before me was a tabula rasa that a dream could be etched upon. I thought of soft grass and hammocks, a fire pit, a pizza oven.

But there was one more thing—for it seemed that there was always one more thing. Removing the bamboo had revealed another abandoned oil tank, this one buried in the ground. A company that does this sort of thing came and drained it, recycling the fuel that had been stagnant in there for many years. Then another company that digs out tanks came. Even my sisters, from their faraway pandemic refuges, became nervous. The removal cost little or a lot depending on whether the tank had a leak or not. It was a five-hundred-gallon tank, solid as an M1 Abrams.

All of this—the septic, the root ball/rhizome removal, the oil tank, the fuel draining, this entire bamboo project—ran about $30,000 and took Sarah and me fifteen months to pay off. We did so with the help of Yolanda's small down payment, countless negative sales, and an assist from the harvesting of the dying ash.

D an, the lumberjack, invited me to a nearby farm so I could see his work. He had harvested a bunch of trees from the owner's forest and thought this might help ease my concerns. "We leave behind the crowns. This will show you what that looks like."

ON A BEAUTIFUL OCTOBER day, I drove the short distance to Easter Farms. There were pumpkins in the yard, gorgeous fall colors, chickens, a rooster crowing, goats, horses. It was perfectly landscaped. A man stooped over a flower bed plucking out weeds. Hard to miss was a giant stack of timber waiting to be priced and hauled to the mill. In front of the well-groomed white clapboard farmhouse, chrysanthemums growing in pots, was a sign that the owners had placed not so much by way of welcome but of warning:

In this house we believe
Freedom of speech
The second amendment
All men and women are equal
Law & Order

Property Rights

All Lives Matter

&

We Stand for our Anthem

We were less than a month from the first national election in United States history in which, as time would continue to reveal in robust and staggering detail, an incumbent president, along with allies in Congress, would attempt to stage a coup d'état. Like the staggering death toll of the pandemic, it was difficult to understand such a thing. As my mother's dementia progressed, a corollary but widespread, virus-like pathology of the mind, delusion, had taken hold across the country. According to the *Diagnostic and Statistical Manual of Mental Disorders*, the thick reference book that psychiatrists and others in the mental health field call the *DSM-5*, delusions "are fixed beliefs that are not amenable to change in light of conflicting evidence. . . . Delusions are deemed bizarre if they are clearly implausible and not understandable to same-culture peers." One could recognize the large-scale form of culture-wide delusion across the ages, and, as one approached the modern era, one recognized it again: in Philippe Henriot, in Goebbels, in Madison Avenue advertising firms, and now in the siloed bubbles of social media.

Daniel Boorstin, in his 1962 book, *The Image: A Guide to Pseudo-Events in America*, identified this danger, calling it "unreality." Trump has been a master of unreality, conjuring up fabrications that a whole swath of people believe in, at great detriment to reality and society. Boorstin called this the greatest menace to our culture—a greater threat than nuclear war, poverty, and economic instability. Boorstin's warning about widespread unreality remained an interesting grad-school seminar topic for decades, until the campaign of the unreal seemed to arrive fully formed. You looked in vain for ways to address it. In the cataclysmic year of 1939, in which Weimar Germany seemed to have lost its collective mind, Carl Jung delivered a lecture in London observing, in a way that Boorstin would echo twenty-three years later, that the greatest global existential risk "was not earthquakes, not microbes, not cancer but man himself who is man's greatest danger . . . for the simple reason that there is no adequate protection against psychic epidemics, which are infinitely more devastating than the worst of natural catastrophes." Unreality could be induced and widely broadcast; the staggering spectacle of the January 6 insurrection was the culmination of a creeping, orchestrated process that might have begun on the day after the 2016 inauguration of Donald Trump, when a White House spokesman threw a public tantrum, saying that the crowd at the Trump inauguration was far bigger than former president Barack Obama's—a statement that was manifestly, unequivocally untrue. The campaign of the unreal continued, as we all know, and by the fall of 2020, you didn't need a weatherman to know which way the weird winds were blowing. In rural Hunterdon County, not far from our road, was a handmade sign in bloodred letters that dripped creepily and said VOTE TRUMP. Twice somebody knocked down our Biden/Harris sign at the foot of the gravel driveway; the second time the culprits took the trouble of knocking down the mailboxes. A roadside stand along Route 202 was doing a booming business in MAGA regalia. Elsewhere, I'd seen an enormous banner with the head of Trump on the body of Rocky Balboa carrying an AK-47. Now I was pulling into the driveway with the preemptively bellicose IN THIS HOUSE yard sign.

I was wearing a mask; Dan and the couple who greeted me were not. I had New York plates on my old BMW. The couple were welcoming, friendly, and showed off the goats immediately. Then Dan pointed out the timber, the ash, the oak, the poplars, estimating the value of the haul (over ten grand), showing me what made it beautiful and valuable.

"She only wants to take out the ash," Dan said to the couple. By this he meant that I was too cautious. He showed me the butts of oak and poplars, explained that that was where the money would be found. The owner was in his sixties, an architect who had grown up on the farm, as had his father and grandfather before him.

"To make a healthy forest you can't be afraid to take down trees," he said. "They have a life span, too." I smiled, thinking of ancient forests that had been around for thousands of years, what that time frame alone can teach us about thinking ahead, about caretaking, about being wise. I've read that tree canopies could be considered the eighth continent for all that's going on up there with epiphytes and birds, that what's going on beneath the ground with mycorrhizae could be considered a ninth continent.

I studied the guy working in the flower bed. The architect told me he traded work with the fellow, a young guy, for hunting. "But he's not for hire," he seemed to warn, holding me with his eyes, all business and some suspicion, like he didn't quite trust me. I wondered what he thought of me. I had read them; surely they had read me, too.

Dan pulled out his phone and showed us a photo of a pretty woman with long brown hair and big brown eyes. "I was telling them," he said to me, "that you look just like my girl." Dan, the lumberjack, unlike the owner, was flirtatious, with a coy smile.

"I'm flattered," I said. "She's pretty." I didn't look anything like her save the brown hair and eyes.

I was about to go into the woods with these guys. Back at the Farm, Mark was working on some songs he was writing with a partner while keeping my mother company. Dayana had the day off and was spending it with Juanpa. Jasper was making Eggs Benedict, a skill he had mastered during lockdown. His school was remote this week. Next week he'd return to New York with Mark for in-person classes. This back-and-forth wasn't working for Jasper. He did well in school, but he was also just waiting for this to all be over, for his life to start. He did what he needed to do, but nothing more.

"The only problem with Dan," the architect said, "is that he's slow. He takes his time. Long and slow. Needs to sleep half the day. He says he's recovering from Lyme's."

Dan stood there with an aw-shucks expression that admitted that *Yes, he was slow, but he was also charming and this couple liked the work he was doing for them so, in turn, I would, too.*

"It's true," the wife said. Then added that they had had the goats seven years. I asked if she milked them, made cheese. "Nope, they're just pets."

"Let's get the show on the road," the architect said. He and Dan went off, pulling up shortly on two ATVs. The wife got on the back of her husband's ATV, and I got on the back of Dan's. I noticed how wet everything was from the rains, and as we raced along a muddy road into the architect's forest, mud splashed up my back. I could feel it hitting me. But somewhere I liked that I was on this adventure, in a foreign country right down the road, the only traveling I'd done in a while. I liked wearing my mask, which had the unanticipated effect of making me feel like a different person, a persona, a spy. The mask made me feel less shy, less reticent. As we sped along, Dan told me to hold on, which meant wrapping my arms around his waist. I did. He picked up speed, the ATV kicking into high gear and racing toward the forest. Somewhere I wanted to be this girl, even if only for a moment. I wrapped my arms around the timber pirate and held on.

THE EASTER FARM FOREST wasn't like ours. There were no invasive species. You could see through the trees for quite a distance. It was well-maintained, with groomed trails for horses. Dan pointed out the downed crowns of the trees he'd cut. He explained that though the crowns got left behind, the trunks were used completely. What isn't worthy of timber is used for phone and electric poles or firewood.

"Would you be comfortable with this," he asked. "Crowns on your forest floor?"

"Honestly, it doesn't look as bad as I'd imagined."

"Hot dog. I knew you'd feel that way," he said, as if he'd won a bet with himself.

Tina had said that tree crowns constituted "debris load," which was good for the forest floor, becoming habitat for creatures too numerous to name—insects, birds, reptiles, flying squirrels, porcupines, the woodland jumping mouse, bats. My timber experiment would be creating just this sort of debris load. Inside of me, I could feel rationalization working in its sneaky, determined way; I'd be doing hero's work, a good thing, yes siree.

After a bit we rode back. Dan spoke about recovering from Lyme and this led to his thoughts about COVID, which to him was a big nuisance. "We can't even sing together at church on Sundays. All these ridiculous rules." As we approached the house, we passed his truck. I noticed a cute dog sitting in the driver seat of the cab, head out the window. "He'll tear you to pieces," he said. The dog had given his friend a bite that needed forty stitches. "He'll tear you to pieces," Dan said again.

THE SNOWS CAME EARLY that winter. It would snow three feet across this pandemic winter. The new owner of the Vieceli place, the guy who rode his dirt bikes in the spring, annoying me, and on whom I called the police to complain about the noise (I confess now) so that he'd quiet down, wasn't who I'd read him to be. Just a young married guy trying to be a good neighbor. He accepted my apology, which was contrite and profuse, and when the snows came, he plowed the driveway, all the way to our front door.

By Thanksgiving, the world had shut down again; schools closed. Livia and Jasper returned full-time to the Farm, moved into their rooms—their schools now fully remote until February. I found a chimney guy who said all that the chimney needed to function was a good cleaning. We made endless fires, which my mother loved, sitting near it, mesmerized by the flames. We bought a Christmas tree and decorated it with strung cranberries and popcorn the way I'd done as a child. On the barn we draped lights so that it glowed at night, a beacon of warmth lighting the way against the bitter cold. The coyotes howled. I loved the Farm; I loved this beautiful world.

Then one day Dan arrived with the prettiest poinsettia I'd ever seen, as if it had been sculpted, three heads on one stem, the beautiful red leaves tucked together, folding in on each other in an intricate design, more like a dahlia in shape than a poinsettia. He also brought his chainsaw, his skitter, his feller buncher, unloading them off the back of another eighteen-wheeler, parking them near the garden in which I'd over-wintered a hundred cloves of garlic and fifty shallots.

In the following days he set to work, starting, at Mark's request, by numbering the harvestable trees with spray paint. They walked the forest together and Dan wrote numbers on the trees. There were over a hundred worthy ash. Mark kept track of the numbered trees with a GPS so we'd be certain only the marked trees were harvested. I said we needed to start by harvesting only a few, increasing the number only if I felt comfortable.

With this business of marking the trees complete, the felling began. As promised, Dan started in the yard. The towering ash, the goalposts for our childhood football games, all ten of us out there rushing, tackling each other, one by one those dead ash came down. It seemed like nothing for Dan. He quickly cut down those giants, the crowns shattering across the lawn, spraying branches everywhere.

"It's called the splash," my father said when I told him what I'd been up to.

Dan was precise and knew how and where to make the trees fall. He sorted the salable timber from the firewood, moving both out of the yard. The firewood poles went to the edge of the former bamboo forest. The timber was stacked near the driveway so that once it was priced and sold it would be easy for the loader to haul away. Cleaning the splash was left to us. This would involve days of work by Jasper, Livia, Mark, and me, raking and more raking, tossing, lifting, piling, stacking, and also many bonfires.

I took Dan around the house and pointed out some other balding, dead ash, asking sweetly if he could just drop them. Even I could tell they were so dead they had no timber value left.

"We want to make mamma happy," he said and cocked a smile. I'm a mamma, I thought, not a girl—realizing the obvious, and that I was so deeply lost in this that I'd even convinced myself I was someone I wasn't.

And then Dan went into the forest.

At the beginning of all this I'd made a deal with him that if I felt uncomfortable at any time, we could stop; we could stop cutting down the trees. I made him swear on his mother that he would take only ash, no other trees, no funny business.

He promised. He swore to God. "And I believe," he said.

If you walk down from the main house, on the right are the two cottages, behind which is a lawn that was once the bamboo forest. Further beyond the cottages is another lawn and in the center of it is the big vegetable garden. Beyond the garden is a massive goat pen, where all the animals lived when we had them. To the left of the pen is a brown-shingled barn, the one we climbed up as kids so that Dan could show us the New York City skyline that wasn't there, the same barn we had strung with Christmas lights. This barn stands next to the driveway. To the right of the goat pen and running alongside it for a stretch is the chicken run, with two small roosting houses where the hens lay their eggs. To the left of this we have our ten-acre field, sloping gently downhill to a pond on the Viecelis' property that my stepfather had convinced Vieceli to dig as a source of water to irrigate the raspberries, which had once grown lusciously in this field. Further to the left, the field abruptly stops, and the forest starts. In Duke's forestry plan, this portion is considered Stand 1, and it contained the largest number of ash. It was in here, therefore, that Dan, the logger, began his harvesting, heading in with his skidder and his chainsaw. He started small, taking down just five trees. Then he invited me to have a look.

I remind you that I was plant blind, like the character in *The Overstory* who doesn't pay attention to trees. But, as I have said, I'd read by now *The Hidden Life of Trees* and also Suzanne Simard's

Finding the Mother Tree. I had, the year before the pandemic, saved the weeping cherry tree by the pool by trimming its roots. I'd been with my sister Jenny as she worried about whether it would survive the root trimming. I'd watched my sophisticated, laconic sister do something that I would not have imagined her ever to do: she pressed her lips to the tree and spoke to it, encouraged it. In time, I watched it regain its strength, as trees can sometimes do whether or not someone has whispered to them. This isn't a story about tree whispering, about how I came to love trees or understand them. It's about something else that had eluded me, about something coming slowly into focus, as slowly perhaps as a tree grows. In my red rain boots and the maroon L.L.Bean winter coat my father gave me for Christmas when I was twelve, a little big so I'd grow into it—I had still not grown into it—I went into the woods and my heart sank. My face went long. Only five trees had been taken, but this little area looked like a bomb had gone off. I counted five stumps. Later, I would ask Mark to check the trees to the records he made on the GPS to see if Dan had taken only five. Okay, I thought. This was bad, but I was new to logging.

Even so, I said, "I don't like the way this looks." I couldn't say anything else.

Dan plucked some sassafras and started chewing on it. "You worry too much," he said. The logger didn't know me very well, but this was not untrue. "You're not worrying about the bats, are you?" No, not bats, but I was thinking about Tina, whom he'd taken to calling the Bat Woman. Yes, Tina had told me a time or two about bats, but she'd warned me that heavy machinery moving through the woods can damage healthy trees, cause erosion, and spread the seeds of the invasives. Along with the downed trees, I saw for the first time what rough work a skidder can do. It had left huge, gash-like tracks everywhere.

What had I got myself into? I was so very far away from fixing up a thing or two. I was deep in the rabbit hole. I was, in fact, buried alive. I had been consumed and it wasn't over.

Using my phone, I took my sister Sarah on a walking tour, but she couldn't see much. She'd received another bill from the excavators, and we needed to make a payment.

Dan dragged the logs out of the forest and cut them into their timber lengths, stacking them for a guy named Norman from a company called Patriot Hardwoods, who would price and buy the timber from my mother's forest, walking the length of each piece, making his assessment, and using a hammer-like device to tag the timber. He came twice—another sweet-talking friendly guy who liked to jaw. He showed me why some ash had more value than others. Dan was always fast to point out the unmistakable tracks of the emerald ash borer snaking the lengths of the logs. On a few logs I didn't see the tracks. I asked about that. Dan said those trees had more value; the borer hadn't made it to them yet. Norman responded by telling Mark and me that he was a poet in his spare time, reciting a poem for us that he carried folded in his wallet. It was a poem about a tree.

Pirates, I thought.

* * *

AFTER THE FIRST CUT, Tina wrote to me to say that one of their trail groomers noticed some poplars had been taken down by the logger. I was mortified. So much for mothers and God. I called Dan to ask him.

"I swore on my mother," he said. "I swore to God, and I believe. I showed you all the logs. They all have borer tracks. You worry too much."

The first haul brought us about $3,200, divided fifty-fifty between logger and landowner.

Dan could tell I was shaken, by the low sum, by the destruction. So to finish the job, he brought in his cousin, and the two of them set into the forest with speed, chainsaws buzzing away followed by the tremendous crashing thud of another tree whose number was up. To say it was an unpleasant sound is to miss a great deal about what I felt. It didn't matter that the trees would die, one way or another, because of the ash borer. When a tree falls in the forest and someone's there to hear it, I can report that the tree makes a sound—a sound that, in its grand, crashing finality, travels in shock waves through the ground and lodges in the heart. A sinking feeling grew in me, keeping me up at night. I had been impatient—a character flaw that my father always worries about. I'd also found a clever way to pay for the whole expensive infrastructure mess. Across my life, I'd developed a reputation, among family and friends, for a certain skill set, a capability, in moments of keen exigence, to conjure some form of a rabbit out of an empty hat. This was one of them, the most intense one of all, but the trick was ruined because I'd clobbered a forest while I was at it.

At night I was haunted by Tina, by my sisters, Jenny hugging the weeping cherry, Laura saving it from the teeth of a chainsaw when Sarah had first wanted to cut it down because of the damage it was causing the pool, Joan asking what I'd done to her childhood forest, Sarah wanting to know if I'd sold more negatives, if the timber would bring in more money.

Then: it was not a windy day. Rather, it was a calm, cold winter day. A crystalline sky. I hadn't slept well, so I slept late but was awoken by the low thud of a tree rumbling to the ground. Then another one. And then another. I wanted to stop Dan. I tried calling him, but he didn't answer. So there: he had the advantage. I wasn't about to venture into the woods with trees crashing down all over the place. I waited, and winced, with each tree fall. I walked to the field for a better view and thought I could see the general area where Dan was working: with each crash, the surrounding trees seemed to jostle and rebound in response, leaning left then right then left again.

What the fuck had I done? That was the only way I could think to put it.

By nightfall, Dan had dragged and stacked an enormous pile of trees by the barn. Norman returned, measured the board feet, assessed the quality, used his little hammer to stamp each piece of timber, wrote a check for $6,000, and left.

After Dan and his cousin had gone, Mark and I took a walk into the forest. The dark canopy of trees gave way to an opening, a clearing, of late winter light that was a tangle of tree crowns, the splash of shattered branches, sawdust, the smell of chainsaw exhaust, and the clean, moon-colored ovals of fresh-cut tree stumps. Lesser, unsellable trees had been felled to make way for the better timber. Dan had barreled the skidder through the forest and gouged a path, churning up dirt that the rains would turn into a muddy mess.

"Christ," my husband said.

Here was a private arena of chainsaw retribution work that didn't require a degree in semiotics to understand: it said, *You're getting paid; deal with this, sweetheart.* It set off a bomb in a crowd and said, *You can't make an omelet without breaking some eggs.* I thought of the bellicose yard sign—"*We stand for the national anthem*"—and the architect who said, "To make a healthy forest you can't be afraid to take down trees." I thought of pickup trucks on Highway 202 with Trump signs and confederate flags tailgating me in my car with New York plates, then barreling past me at full throttle, only to come to a stop at the next red light just ahead, where, it seemed, we'd both sit at the intersection, simmering with rage. I thought about Aussie Bob's suggestion that maybe I should stock up on ammunition. I thought of children being held in cages at the border, the casual cruelty of it. I thought of the police officer who murdered George Floyd—how, as he used his knee to choke the life out of the man, a video showed the officer casually put his hands in his pockets, as if he were just killing time. In the months to come, an epidemic of poisonings would occur across the country among people who believed it was better to ingest a cattle deworming agent than to receive a COVID vaccine.

A pandemic of unreality was laced with an undertow of menace that could erupt at any intersection, any parking lot. I thought of our Zombie Apocalypse game. The gash in our forest, as big as three football fields, a big muddy mess left behind, was a score-settling act that reminded me of the mailboxes that the vandals had knocked down at the foot of our driveway along with our BIDEN FOR PRESIDENT sign. I felt like a complete fool, my mind racing in a belated, lacerating, hand-to-forehead flash of the obvious, my mind in triage mode. I thought of all the hikers, I thought of Tina, my sisters, my stepfather even, haunting me from his grave.

When Dan returned for more chainsaw work in the forest, I told him we were finished.

"I've been doing this since I was a teenager," he said. I knew this. He had told me this, cutting down trees since he was a kid. "And no one, not one person, has ever sent me away from a job." All the sweet charm and sassafras was gone. His handsome face turned mean. He couldn't look at me. He packed up his machinery and was gone. All the "firewood poles" he'd cut down, dozens upon dozens of poles, lay strewn about the former bamboo forest. Dan once said that I should write a novel about how great logging is, how it's a miracle of the forest, how you take out trees, you harvest trees, you make money on trees, and just like that they return—bigger, taller, more beautiful than before. He said I could follow the life of a felled tree, how it goes from aging, being old in the forest, on death's door, to becoming a baseball bat for a kid who uses it to hit a home run. "It's life in action," he said. "A bestseller."

Wrapped in furry blankets, Livia, Jasper, Mark, and I took

pictures of the logs waiting for pickup in the yard. There was something surreal about them, also something sad. "Why did we do this?" my daughter asked.

"To help pay for the new septic for the cottages," I said, feeling defeated.

"There's always something to pay for," Jasper said, a bit of disdain in his voice. He'd come to hate this place, the Farm.

In the morning, two eighteen-wheelers pulled up the long driveway and the great pile of priced and cut timber—the furniture, flooring, doors, cabinetry, architectural molding, tool handles, and baseball bats of a bestseller I will leave someone else to write—were gone.

I was telling this story to Frankie, one of the recreational hunters who paid us to hunt deer on our property. I'd felt bad about making such a mess of the forest for them. Dan's equipment had smashed one of Jeff's tree stands. I offered them a season of hunting for free. I also told them, guiltily, about the idea of a management hunter, as Tina had suggested we needed—that Jeff and Frankie would have competition. There seemed to me no end to the mistakes that I had made with my brilliant ash tree harvest. Jeff and Frankie took the news in stride, accepted my offer of a free season, and even offered to help clean up the mess Dan had left behind, chopping up the trees into firewood.

"Where did Norman take the lumber?" Frankie asked me. He had a professional interest in the question, as he worked for a tree removal and landscaping company and had been a good, reliable source of information about many things and especially all things related to trees, their removal, the hazards thereof, the replanting of saplings and the like.

I mentioned Pennsylvania, maybe Canada, but wasn't exactly sure.

"That's illegal," Frankie said. "Ash aren't allowed to leave the county. That's how the borer travels."

Add that to the bestselling novel about baseball bats, I thought, thinking also of those emerald ash borers hitching another ride, perhaps even launching themselves, merrily, off the back of a logging truck barreling down a highway to untouched forests of ash in Pennsylvania or Canada.

There was, as the mounting evidence seemed to indicate, a lot I didn't know. I grew up at the edge of a forest that I had never cared to explore. Perhaps, more generously, I'd been afraid of it. I hadn't understood its magic until my kids took me on those hikes, until the people escaping the confines of their lockdowns ventured across our field, stumbled upon our garden, until I met Tina and even Duke, until I blew a four-acre hole in Stand 1.

I would learn that small family-owned forests ranging in size from one to a hundred acres make up 38 percent of forests in the United States—a sizable swath of trees that, in total, account for a wildlife area of carbon-sequestering forest half-again bigger than the size of Texas. I would learn that most of the people who own these forests are like me: they are blind, think their forests will take care of themselves. If they are wiser, see the problem, there is only so much they can do about it, as forest management requires access to expertise and resources. It's expensive to take care of forests.

Now that I had done a good job of decimating a portion of ours, what came flooding in was shame and an urgency to understand how I could fix the mess I had made. In the beginning, shame triumphed.

I couldn't sleep, dread overcoming me at three a.m. I would spend those dark hours googling what I could and should do, becoming quickly overwhelmed by all the information. I'd been stupid. Whoever anywhere likes to be stupid?

Then Tina emailed. It was time once again for her to make a visit. The dread deepened. Tina of the bats, the Bat Lady. I set a date with her for our walk through the forest. It was January. The kids were still at the Farm, their schools still remote. It was cold and gray. We'd recently celebrated New Year's Eve, making toasts and spilling dreams about all that we would do when this pandemic was finally over. Jasper couldn't wait to be back in New York City. Livia wished that her senior year would include in-class learning and an actual graduation. Dayana and Juanpa were isolating in the basement because a trip to her mother had exposed them to COVID. We passed champagne to Dayana through the sliding door. All of us took care of Mom during Dayana's fourteen-day quarantine.

As the day approached for Tina's visit, I kept imagining, usually at three a.m., her sweet face distorted by horror as she looked upon what I'd done.

On the morning of her visit, it occurred to me that I had somewhere else to be. I needed to get something from a store somewhere, I said, and I told Mark, over my shoulder, in passing, that Tina might come while I was gone. I knew damn well that Tina was coming, in her little neon orange hat and her holstered clippers, and I knew—there were some things I did know—that I had no intention of being there to greet her. That's what husbands are for.

As I fled down Gulick Road, I passed her pickup with the D&R logo and all its promise of saving and preserving land. I stayed away for a long time, just sitting in my car feeling bad. Mark tried calling but I didn't pick up.

I have a long relationship with fear and fault, fear that I've done something wrong, that it (whatever *it* is) is all my fault. I could list any number of things—placing myself in Dan's bed, for instance, that getting up and leaving too fast would make him feel bad. The relationship extends to lesser events—the two different shoes I wore to school on occasion were because I'd lost the mates. We needed to repaint the swimming pool. Dan had a notion all of us would paint our own small sea creature. Mine was an enormous octopus, so big and ugly that it not only had to be painted over, the entire pool also needed to be repainted. All my fault. I felt guilty all the time, like I had stolen something, was bad. My stepmother used to buy clothes for me that I could only keep at my father's house, that I couldn't take with me to the Farm because they would get lost there. The clothes were fun, like nothing my mother would buy me—polyester short shorts, a turquoise T-shirt with a shooting star made of rhinestones. I loved Elton John and his flamboyant wardrobe, so Yolanda bought me kid things that nodded to that style. I also loved pretty dresses, long fancy party gowns, hoopskirts out of *Gone with the Wind*, velvet and taffeta, silk. Yolanda was a talented seamstress, and she made these fantasies come true on her sewing machine. I liked to wear the fancy dresses and pretend that I was Scarlett or Cathy from *Wuthering Heights*. When my grandmother visited, I'd implore her to twist my hair with rags at night so that in the morning I'd have sausage curls. All this, it made me feel like I had some control, that the dresses and the curls could make me feel normal. I liked to pretend my stepbrother Tony, a year younger than I with long curly dark hair, was Heathcliff because I loved Tony very much and wanted a spectacular narrative with him. When he was eight and I was nine, I made a deal with him. If he was my servant for a day, did everything I said for an entire day, I'd be his servant on the following day. I wore a fancy dress and ordered him around. The next day, my turn to do for him, all that wild hair and those big innocent blue eyes, looked at me to start serving him. I laughed. "Do you think I'm stupid," I said. Somehow, I was getting revenge on fear and fault. I wanted to feel what power felt like.

After a short time, I couldn't take any of what Yolanda gave me to the Farm because at the Farm it was sucked into some mysterious void where it permanently disappeared. And it was always all my fault. Her solution was to have me leave the clothes at Drake's Corner Road, so I could see that they wouldn't disappear, that they would be right where I left them when I next returned. And they were, and she was trying to teach me something, but it didn't quite work. I was mad that I couldn't keep the clothes with me, embarrassed that I'd lose them at the Farm because I wasn't attentive enough, as if the Farm ate things.

And there was something else that was my fault, my parents' divorce. It was my fault. If I'd have been more worthy, it wouldn't have happened. This was only intuitive, not conscious—an invisible part of my nervous system.

It seemed to reason that if everything was my fault, it redounded to me to fix it.

I IMAGINED MARK AND Tina walking through the woods, eventually coming upon the bombed-out area with all its shattered crowns. Tina's eyes would be drawn to the pale, fresh-cut tree stumps among the wreckage, the corduroy patterns of the tree rings, the many decades of time each tree holds within itself, now exposed in the impugning wash of sunlight, churned-up earth and wind. I tried to imagine what Tina would be thinking. I imagined nature lovers on a hike coming upon this scene. I imagined their shock and disappointment. I imagined them shaking their heads and turning back or turning uphill to walk through the scene of the crime. I imagined the Instagram photos they'd post of the logging damage, the complaints they'd file to D&R Greenway. I imagined the D&R trail crews, all volunteers, who had spent many hot summer days lugging heavy irons suitable for moving boulders and native slate to build the beautiful stone bridges and steps that made the trail so magical—I imagined them coming upon this blasted clearing, with its wide gashes made by the timber pirate's logging skidder, and I braced myself for what Tina would be saying to Mark as he tried to call me and I sat there in the parking lot of a hardware store refusing to answer. Tina's eyes: I could see them all the way from Flemington, scanning the scene, perhaps looking for new-cut timber suitable for making a pillory for me, which could then be placed conveniently by the trail, my head and hands locked in wooden stocks fashioned by the trees I had murdered, in honor of the bats I had displaced, and the ash borers I'd disbursed, where people could take more Instagram photographs of the person who had caused all of this woodland destruction.

Tina's visits were usually a couple of hours. When those hours had passed, I went home.

Mark was waiting for me. He asked where I'd been and why I hadn't called. I told him. He laughed. "You've got it all wrong," he said.

Tina, it turns out, did not lower the boom, but helped him understand what would be involved in restoring "The Clearing." That became the euphemism, the term of art we used when we spoke of the logged swath of forest. At first it only eased the sting of the disaster, but it would soon register a growing aspiration forming in our hearts—for the entire forest itself, most of which had remained untouched.

That "untouched" quality, Tina pointed out, was, surprisingly, part of the wider problem that she had already started speaking with me about, that Duke had spoken with me about. Unlike Duke, Tina was not a pessimist. Dan the logger had done a lot of damage, true enough. In his haste to get down as many trees as possible and then get the logs out he'd been careless with his machinery, driving it any which way that made for the speediest route, leaving skid tracks everywhere, banks of dirt a few feet high, plowing into healthy trees— oaks and poplars—and leaving gaping wounds. But Tina had some solutions. The first order of business was to seed the skid tracks with native grasses and flowers to prevent erosion. The second was to engage a management hunter to suppress the deer. Deer gobbled acorns, denuded saplings, leaving little chance that a healthy understory could emerge. Then came the third order of business—finding affordable ways to eradicate the non-native plants, those delicious wineberries we collected for jams, the fragrant honeysuckle we sucked the sweet juices from as kids. They were slowly turning the forest floor into a thorny, selfish, monocultural fortress of light hoarders that choked young saplings and other native plants that the deer didn't finish off first. The fourth order of business, with the invasives cleared and the deer suppressed, would be to plant and then tend and protect the saplings, to rebuild the understory. This would be an enormous undertaking, expensive, impossible for one person or even a few people. But I started thinking about it. My idea was to start small, begin with the Sandy Stand and then, if I succeeded, I would move on to the area of the forest Dan had decimated, Stand 1.

In the middle of the night when I couldn't sleep, I googled the various steps. I started with the management hunter and found a local guy named Brian. I wrote to him, and he wrote right back. He made a career of clearing deer, donating the meat to a food bank. He told me that I'd need to speak to Jeff and Frankie, the recreational hunters, before he could hunt our land.

I contacted Jeff and Frankie. They understood our predicament. They didn't mind sharing the hunting with Brian. Things were looking up. I felt something new. It wasn't just a sense of purpose and curiosity. It wasn't just a new target, a task for me to tackle or fix.

This was different. It did not spring like a rabbit from a hat. It did not come from a sense of desperation or five-alarm-fire decision-making. I needed a word or phrase for this new thing, this good thing, but nothing came readily to mind. It wasn't the proverbial calm after a storm—but it was calm—or calming—and not being a calm person by any stretch of the imagination, this caught my attention. This was something big. This was something new. Maybe "big" provided a clue to what it was, this calm I began to feel.

Mark had told me about a moment in the locked-down COVID spring of 2020, in late March, when buds were forming on the trees and a day could sometimes be, despite the wind, if you lay down on the ground for a moment, in a coat, as he did, and watched the dogs cavort in the tall grass, and if you listened to the wind rise and fall in the forest—such a day could feel almost sunny and warm. On one such day, Mark had walked with the dogs past the chicken coop and along the south edge of a fence line that followed the big ten-acre field east of the main house and the garden. We'd fantasized about planting rows of lavender in that field. It wasn't out of the realm of possibility. Farmers planted lavender in New Jersey. To get out of the wind, Mark had lain down, in his coat, and watched the woods. He'd been married to me for almost twenty-five years. He'd been coming to the Farm with me longer than that, a witness to the spectacle that my family could sometimes be—he knew my stepfather, my grandmother, the fights I could get into with my sisters. On our wedding day, for her speech, Joan raised her glass to Mark and said, laughing, and by way of familial embrace, "You can't ever say that you didn't know what you were getting into." Mark understood the stories, knew about all the baggage, or most of it, and mostly because of this he had always felt, like almost everyone else did, that the Farm, for as beautiful as it was, had a strange, brittle weirdness about it, contained too many ghosts, too many stories that too many people just wanted to forget. Being at the Farm had always made him feel as if he were living inside a Chekhov or Ibsen play, a play that takes place in a threadbare, tumbled-down estate with a family gathered, all the old grudges and grievances unsheathed, the conversations filled with knives and stabbing jokes, all of this against the backdrop of societal upheaval taking place beyond their world. Because of this, Mark had always kept the Farm at an emotional distance. But lying just out of the wind in the sun and looking at the trees and the field that could be lavender, he said the size of his life seemed very small, and the size and scope of the forest seemed suddenly to dwarf any family drama, any human drama, any human who might have ever passed this way at any time in history or prehistory. He squinted in the sun to watch the play of the wind in the trees. Against that scale of time, we were nothing. It was like standing next to a mountain and understanding how little anything that ever happened to you mattered or would ever matter to anyone. And somehow, this perspective was deeply calming for him . . . and then for me, too, as I became engaged with ideas of aiding the forest. He recalled this moment of his, lying in the field, studying the forest, giving it to me as a sort of invitation. It wasn't acquiescence. It wasn't something out of Schopenhauer. It had the opposite effect one might expect.

I recognized something in Mark's story. A calm settled over me, too, born of curiosity, as we began to shoulder the notion of restoring the forest. I wasn't worried about the project's colossal scale. It both made me feel more alive and gave me a new understanding of what I could be doing here—and by "here" I began to mean, increasingly, that portion of time and place I had been allotted on this earth, how tiny that was, how little one person could do, but also that this was a recognition of proper—that is to say, sane—and manageable limits. It wasn't a limitation to recognize limits. It was, in fact, liberating. It would not fall to me or to my husband alone to solve this problem. We would face it, and join with others, perhaps our children and relatives, our friends, my sisters, and we would begin the slow, good work of restoration. It would take place across many lifetimes. It was good to do, and it was good to begin. I kept thinking of the famous opening of the *Joy of Cooking*, that tome of human wisdom about food and cuisine, which at the outset offers a helpful, practical moment of orientation for the reader to the colossal task at hand: *Stand facing the stove.*

THE KIDS HOME AGAIN from school, vaccinated now in the late spring of 2021 but still at the Farm, I'd engage the family with the forest. My daughter had a remote internship and decided she preferred being at the Farm to being in the city. She could see her grandmother's decline and she wanted to be near her. Jasper came out from New York only under duress. Eventually, we would (unwisely) surrender and allow him to stay in the city—often alone. On one occasion, when we were all together, I took them through the forest to show them what I'd been up to. They offered to help. We went into the bombed-out clearing. We took with us a chainsaw and a machete and other tools, spent about an hour cutting vines, clearing multiflora rose and other prickly, snarling vine-choking branches, autumn olive whose sole purpose, it seems, is to block the sun from young saplings. We dragged the felled debris out of the woods and stacked it into a pile, and when we were done, sweating and tired, if you stepped back for a look, you could see a newly cleared patch of woods no bigger than a living room with three baby oak saplings gleaming in the sun. If the four of us kept at it for forty hours a week, we might clear an acre in a little less than a week. The forest was thirty-five acres. If we were lucky, and invasives had taken over only half of the forest (where the canopy is thickest, the invasives are less abundant for lack of light), it would still take a team of four people working full-time close to six months to do the job, and only if the conditions were right. (That is, if my math is correct.) *Stand facing the stove.*

Until then, I would apply for grants, I would give my time, get my children and husband more involved, my sisters (I hoped). My son, the recalcitrant seventeen-year-old, thought up a business plan, considered a GoFundMe page, did some research himself, ordered saplings he intended to plant—even he, lost in the pandemic, found a purpose for himself when circumstance forced him to be at the Farm.

It occurred to me as well that perhaps this kind of work, repairing small private forests, could present opportunities, at a scale half again as large as Texas, for local, state, and federal government agencies to help private landowners like my mom whose forests were endangered but who lacked the means to do anything about it. Against a backdrop of recent economic projections that automation will destroy up to 54 million American jobs in the next ten years, government partnerships could bring to life a latent but substantial forest management and restoration industry—part of a Green New Deal including wind, solar, transmission line construction, energy efficiency, and land management that included forest restoration, creating jobs and stimulating local economies for millions of people. It occurred to me, in other words, that my attempt to put my mom's forest back on a healthy footing could become a way of talking about this larger societal and ecological imperative.

The point, I came to see, is that we can't afford *not* to save such forests, which are spectacularly powerful agents of carbon sequestration, a key feature of greenhouse gas mitigation, and are projected to deliver up to a third of the carbon reductions needed by 2030. While the climate battle will be on many fronts, without forests—without the healthy, billowy, soft machines of carbon sequestration—we cannot hope to solve the problem of climate change. Small forests like Mom's are collectively projected to sequester nearly a billion tons of carbon annually. That number could be increased dramatically with bold policy decisions in Congress—if more private landowners had access to carbon markets, as they do in California, or were otherwise incentivized. Come what may, we cannot hope to leverage the sequestering soft engines of forests without incentivizing small landowners to help keep forests healthy for generations to come.

You scratch the surface, in other words—you answer the call to fix something broken in your mom's house—and an entire ecosystem shudders and wobbles and swings into view, and yet the thread connecting healthy trees to healthy economies also emerges in a way one never would have guessed. And that thread (my mind was swelling with possibility, carrying me right out of myself and my own minuscule smallness) expands and extends to one of the largest concerns of our nation and the world, global warming, and how a forest, saving a forest, is part of the solution.

ON ONE OF THOSE camping trips with my father and Jenny so long ago, I woke up in the middle of the night crying. We were in a tent, the three of us. I shook my father to wake him. He asked me what was wrong. I was sobbing. We had recently left Yolanda and her children after a month together on a lake in New Hampshire. Now we were alone in the woods with news of bear attacks, our food strung up high in a tree. "I miss Yolanda," I said. I felt, as I was saying the words, that I was lying, trying to make my father feel okay that I was sad and crying. I didn't want him to know that I was simply scared, missing my mother in the deep deep woods so very far away from everywhere. Yet at the same time, I really did miss Yolanda, but felt guilty for missing her, as if I were betraying my mother. Layer upon layer of deceit and truth. I was ten or eleven, a young kid, but I already understood well what could be said to one parent and not the other. My father held me close in his arms and let me cry. And I did. I cried and cried. I think he cried, too. He was moved that I missed Yolanda, happy that I missed Yolanda.

If I came to see my engagement with the trees, my burgeoning curiosity for understory development as a path to higher purpose, as a deepening of all the reasons I'd come up with for why I was here—pandemic, mother, correction of the past, a second chance at motherhood at the moment when my children were on the cusp of adulthood—I got here, to these trees and this forest, in part because Yolanda gave us the seed money necessary to fix the septic. She was the initial stepping stone into the forest and to a kind of lightness and exhilaration I hadn't felt in a very long time.

You grow up, you get old, you forgive. You realize we are all human. Can't it be that simple? The Greeks say, *Know thyself.* The quest is in there. Yolanda and my father fell in love when they were still married to others. Their choice was another stepping stone, leading away from a safe white house in the woods to an ever-expanding chaos. Somewhere along the way, the effects of their choices became incorporated into the fabric of who I am. The same can be said for Mom. I had not been able to stay angry at her. I met Dan at the Abbey Pub because that was the stepping stone back to my mother and I wanted to get back with my mother. Somewhere across the years I forgave her—for staying with Dan, for enduring his abuse, for not protecting me, for not understanding I was terrified of that basement bedroom with the ghosts hidden by rabbits, for not seeing me, that I was terrified as a child. Why? Because I love her, because I, too, am imperfect, because she, too, was hurt, because she loved me and still loves me though she has no idea who I am, because she is my mother.

And Dan? The question of my second novel, *Gorgeous Lies*, was about why we continue to love people who hurt us. I haven't read the novel since I wrote it some twenty years ago, so I don't know if I solved that riddle. I doubt it.

Dan could have been a spectacular man. He had a brilliant aesthetic eye, a big imagination, a playful, curious self. He wanted to be good, do right, live creatively on his own terms. Goodness was important to him. And he was loved, is loved. But he, too, was hurt and afraid, and that fear turned into rage and the consequence was ours.

There is a different version of the Farm out there.

There is a different version of me—the other me raised by intact parents, the other me raised by the spectacular version of Dan.

Couldn't we all be spectacular, if only?

How long can you stay angry at something or someone without becoming the anger?

I CALLED DUKE. I had an idea. The Sandy Stand, as we called it, the area that had been decimated by the storm in 2012 and that had no understory whatsoever, no emerging trees, just brambles, would be my proof-of-concept test site. If I could help along an understory here, in this relatively small area, I could move on to the clearing with my new expertise. I told Duke that I wanted to remove the invasives and then fill it with saplings. I told him that I had engaged a management hunter and that I was working on eradicating the invasives. If I succeeded in this one area, I would move on to other areas. Bit by bit I'd save this forest. I think I wanted to impress him. I think I wanted him to praise me and say, *well done* and *go for it* and *I'll help.*

"It would take an army," Duke said. I didn't flinch.

"I'm starting small," I said.

"Be my guest," he said, and this is where he dared me. "Most of my clients fail. They get big ideas and then they fail. I'm retiring. It's not a good time to be a forester."

I persisted.

He told me where to place an order for native saplings and he directed me to two videos on YouTube that he'd made about planting saplings and then transplanting them into the forest. The idea was to start the saplings in your garden, near a water source in any case, pop them in the ground, allow them to grow for a season or two so they could get above deer-grazing height. Being near a water source allowed for more control. The summers can be hot and dry here. When the saplings are left alone in the forest they can die from thirst. And if thirst doesn't kill them, the deer do. He suggested I start with sugar maples because they are fast growing. "Most of my clients who have tried this have failed, too," he said. It was time for him to retire. I was not going to fail.

"Why?" I asked.

"Because they forget to water the trees," he said.

"I won't forget to water the trees."

I ordered fifty sugar maple saplings, starting small, facing the stove.

"*Acer saccharum*," my father said when I told him what I was doing. "Life span as long as two hundred to three hundred years."

AS I TOLD DUKE I would do, I hired some men I couldn't afford, slipping further into debt, and had them help me clear the Sandy Stand. It was January of 2021 and the guys who helped me were seasonally unemployed landscape workers, as this wasn't a season known for landscaping work. With machetes and shovels they started removing the invasive shrubs. I also had them rake out the rocks from the former bamboo forest so that I could seed it with grass in the spring. Those rocks of Rocktown—my father was still looking into them and had made a date with Linc the petrologist to study the specimen I'd left with him. "Unusual rocks," Dad had recently told me, picking up the thread again. His house, ten miles down the road from the Farm, sat on the same exact rock, but it wasn't broken up at his house the way it was in Rocktown. On the agreed-upon day, I drove Dad, and the rocks, to Linc for a petrology lesson. Linc greeted us with a big friendly smile and a special hammer for breaking up the samples, which he immediately did, showing me their insides as they easily came apart. I won't give the lesson here that Linc gave to me, because I'll get it wrong, but I did love standing in Linc's driveway with my father, listening to the words—columnar basalt, liquid magma, diabase, palisades sill.

For our birthdays, in the years after the divorce, my father would give my sisters and me hundred-dollar days—days in which we could spend a hundred bucks as long as we spent it with him. We could choose whatever we wanted to do, and he'd arrange it. The word *Palisades* always reminds me of being about six years old on a hundred-dollar day at an amusement park called the Palisades in the Palisades. The name alone made me think of castles. The amusement park had an enormous waterslide that I slid down with Dad again and again and again. When I wasn't on the slide I was on his shoulders, hoping I could stay there forever, that I would never get too big for his shoulders.

Somehow, I understood from Linc and my broken-up samples that though the rocks in Princeton and Ringoes are the same, they formed differently when cooling so many millions of years ago. The fissures in the rocks at the Farm were closer together than in Princeton, so they broke up more easily and into smaller pieces in the weathering process, hence all the small rocks that I was determined to get rid of so that I could seed the former bamboo forest with grass. If I could mow the cleared area, I could keep any renegade bamboo at bay, essential to making sure that it did not return. One stray rhizome or root ball needed only a bit of time to multiply and return a full army. When I got the bill for the two weeks of work, three men, I had to abandon the effort. Half the area, though, of both the bamboo and the Sandy Stand, had been prepared and a small mountain of rocks had been moved.

In the days before I realized I couldn't afford the men, they started two bonfires to get rid of the debris. One was small and manageable and the other was large and, they insisted, also manageable. I had gone out and came back to see smoke billowing into the sky. That evening, Bill, the tenant in the lower cottage, called me to register his concern. "That's a very big fire," he said. It was about a twenty-five-foot-wide circle, and the debris included the rhizome root ball hill and also the uprooted stumps of two ash, many of the poles abandoned by Dan, the logger. The workers had kept piling it on. They assured me that the weather was conducive, no windstorms on the horizon. Even so this was an epic bonfire. It would burn for days. For days I would worry that the helicopters and low-flying planes that seemed to be circling overhead were the police—that old fear of Dan's about police spying on his pot from above, descending on ropes. I thought the neighbors would say something. I worried about the damage to the environment, that once again I was contributing hook, line, and sinker to the mess.

I read about fires on the internet. They are illegal. But I also learned that New Jersey had recently changed the laws so that private property owners with invasive species problems could apply to the state for prescribed burns. I wrote to Tina to ask her what she thought. She liked the idea. I applied for a prescribed burn. I also applied to burn debris, a burn permit. I was so far down the rabbit hole, and it was kind of cool down here. I was learning things about the land upon which I stood, solving some problems—or at least felt that I was untangling chaos, that I was trying.

* * *

THE STATE OF NEW Jersey offered a program that landowners with invasive species problems could apply for, the Environmental Quality Incentives Program. I applied. A woman named Jess drove out from her offices in Frenchtown and I took her on a hike, told her my ideas, what I wanted to accomplish, showed her the underpopulated Sandy Stand, explained that I was going to use that as my testing ground for creating an understory, that I'd be raising saplings in the paddock, moving them after they went dormant. She explained the next steps in the application process, cautioned that it would take a long time. I proceeded.

Late at night, now I was excited when I couldn't sleep. I quickly discovered the Yale School of the Environment's magazine, *Yale Environment 360*. The first article I read was titled "How Small Family Forests Can Help Meet the Climate Challenge," written by Gabriel Popkin and published June 4, 2020. Recent stuff. The subtitle reads:

As efforts grow to store more CO_2 emissions in forests, one sector has been overlooked—small, family-owned woodlands, which comprise 38 percent of U.S. forests. Now, a major conservation initiative is aiming to help these owners manage their lands for maximum carbon storage.

Back in April 2020, on the threshold of the pandemic, three environmental nonprofits—the Nature Conservancy, American Forest Foundation, and Vermont Land Trust—announced two new programs "powered by a $10 million rocket boost from the tech giant Amazon, to funnel funds from carbon emitters to small landowners . . . eager to grow larger, healthier forests."

From the Nature Conservancy, "Family Forests: An Untapped Powerhouse in Climate Mitigation": "Over the past several years, there has been a renewed conversation around the efforts to improve the sustainability of forests. All too often, these small landowners have been excluded from the national climate change conversation and the opportunity to participate in the carbon credit market, which could both provide families with sustained revenue and bring meaningful climate change mitigation practices to fruition."

In those midnight hours, I read lots of things, articles with names like "My Healthy Woods" or "How Non-Native Plants Are Contributing to a Global Insect Decline" or "Regenerating Hardwood Forests: Managing Competing Plants, Deer, and Light."

I felt lifted. Perhaps I could find funding, support? My brief engagement with the three workers for two weeks had cost more than $3,000. If there was foundational assistance, I imagined what I might accomplish. I had already noted that the invasives weren't everywhere. They were thickest closest to the house, but as you went farther into the woods, they petered out because there was better canopy cover, less light. The job was smaller than it had at first appeared. All thirty-five acres of forest had not been invaded.

But whoever gives money away easily? Searching the various sites, I learned that funding either wasn't available in New Jersey or that there was some other insurmountable hurdle. So, while I kept searching for funding sources, kept reading about forests, I also continued with the steps that had been clearly set out for me by Tina and Duke.

In early February 2021, my family left again, one by one—Livia back to in-person college, Jasper and Mark back to New York. There were stretches in which I was alone at the Farm with my mother, Dayana, and Juanpa. It was cold and dark. Two feet of snow was on the ground and more kept coming. Mom colored. Dayana worked on her business. I taught. Juanpa went to school and when at home put together complex puzzles easily. He also played video games endlessly on a television in the basement. I was at the Farm, unable to leave, telling myself I had projects I needed to stay on top of, concerning myself with the forest. It still wasn't easy to come and go without worrying about COVID, bringing it back to my mother. Meanwhile, Dayana and her son still needed to be relieved on the weekends. My sisters were still in their own COVID shelters Elsewhere. So, I stayed; I wanted to stay; I never wanted to leave. In the evenings, I made dinner for Mom, Dayana, and Juanpa. The four of us would sit around the table and try to find things to say, talking about Juanpa's school, the rapid progress he was making with English, Mom distracted by our reflections in the glass, believing there were people outside who wanted to get in.

After most of us had gone off to college and our adult lives, Mom took in an entire family from Trenton. The kids stayed frequently at the Farm; Mom drove the mother to school so she could get her high school diploma. Mom had big plans for the family, intended to get each child into a "good" college. She arranged for them to have after-school activities, go to summer camp in Vermont. She bartered with the camp, offering her talents as a photographer in exchange for tuition. There were five kids total, siblings and cousins. I didn't pay much attention at the time—just one of Mom's things, trying to save so many lives. That's the way I see it. Mom wanted to do good work, help people out, but there was also a desire to be a savior, to treat others the way she wanted to be treated herself. In return, she wanted to be saved by their kindness and love. But who really wants to be saved, what does that even mean? The obligation becomes a burden. As a result, Mom's efforts never ended well for her; she never felt saved. Rather she could feel like a victim, that she'd been treated poorly after doing so much.

When my sisters and I were young, those first years at the Farm, Mom was more interested in saving Dan's children than saving us. She favored them, doted on them, trying to secure their love because she knew that ours was already safe. It was the same with the family from Trenton. I suppose it made Mom feel powerful, worthy, filled something inside, lacquered over the chaos—or contributed to it so that she didn't have to think about herself, her circumstances and choices. And she was doing good works. These people wanted her, needed her; she was going to make their worlds bigger, their lives better. It gave her a sense of self that she was missing; it made her feel important and good. But like all the strangers who appeared and stayed for years, the story didn't end as she initially intended. Time moved her away from them, the family from Trenton, with some of the kids staying in touch now and again. It didn't end badly, but it wasn't a panacea either, the way these things rarely are.

At the dinner table in that cold February, as we approached the anniversary of the world closing down, watching the reflections in the dining room glass as we ate the meal that I had cooked, thinking of Mark and Jasper in New York, I wondered what I was doing here once again. A terrifying thought occurred to me: I'd become my mother. I was trying to keep this family (Mom, Dayana, Juanpa) going at the expense of my son and husband. They would certainly have liked it if I'd been with them. It was an awful thought that stabbed through me until I pushed it away. I could not dwell there. I still wasn't vaccinated, I reminded myself, going back and forth unvaccinated wasn't a possibility, how would I relieve Dayana, I asked myself. Very little in life is so tidy. I never told myself that this wasn't my responsibility, that if I left someone else might step in.

In the mornings, increasingly Mom would resist Dayana's attempts to get her into the shower. From my room, where I prepared to teach, I could hear Mom scream: "Help me, help me." So I'd go and help. Sometimes Mom would say that Dayana was trying to kill her. I knew this wasn't the truth. She said it about me, too. Mom would be standing there naked, her breasts hanging like two enormous eggplants, her beautiful slender legs strong stems supporting her drooping body. I hated her naked body. I hated the Depends, the wipes, the surgical gloves, the smell of her, the decay of her, the nakedness of her, but I could not leave. Who would help Dayana if I wasn't there? What would Dayana do when Mom screamed for help if I wasn't there? Dayana would quit if I wasn't there. The idea of Dayana quitting terrified me. I'd take Mom's arm and gently lead her to the shower, soothing her with "It's all right."

BRIAN, THE DEER HUNTER, came in February. He came three times to hunt and as many to bait. There were monumental snows, but he came anyway. I saw him, from the dining room window, walk straight across the front lawn and down into the woods behind the pool. On his first visit he wasn't five minutes into the woods before I heard the boom of a shot, later two more, more distant. When he was finished, he wrote me:

I saw 15 deer tonight I was able to shoot 3 that's all the dragging energy I had. The snow is still very deep down in the woods. Thanks again for allowing me to management hunt on your property. Sorry about the dogs barking.

The next time he came, I didn't see him go in, but I did see him come out. He was trudging through the snow, dragging a dead doe. He got it across the lawn to his truck in the parking area and then headed back for another and then another.

I'm an opportunist hunter, take what is presented to you. Because I shot two with one shot, they scattered. I knew they would come back within an hour because they're extremely

hungry with the snow and that's when 10 of the earlier group
came back and I was able to get the third one but then they
really took off.

The does were pregnant, each with two babies. He'd been here
just a few times, in the heavy snow, and he'd cleared twelve deer if
you count the babies. Why wouldn't you count the babies? The way I
had come to think about deer—as antlered rats—mildly shocked me,
shocked me some more when I'd see them, I'd see them everywhere,
in packs coming up the driveway at dusk, dead by the side of the
road, lurking from the woods, their eyes chatoyant. When we drive
nearing the Farm, my kids tend to shout out when they see white-
tails in the fields, sometimes accompanied by spotted fawns.

"Oh, look at the deer!" they say.

"I wish I had a gun," I say.

"Mom!" they shout.

I don't know what I'd do with a gun. I do know there was nothing
cute about the deer.

After Brian's last visit and a flurry of questions from me, he wrote:

The does were roughly 85 to 95 pounds, probably 2$\frac{1}{2}$ 3$\frac{1}{2}$ years
old. From a meat standpoint you get about 38% of the total
body weight which is edible and is how they figure the formula.
When you donate a deer it provides 200 meals.

    Feel free to ask as many questions as you want. The more
you understand the better it is for management hunting. And

it is extremely hard work. I am physically whooped. I've taken 213 deer this deer season and I'm just about mentally done. But it's my thing.

REGARDING DAN, I HADN'T understood why Joan was mad at me and hadn't spoken to me for close to a year. In those early days, I'd heard through the sister vine that she was mad, but I couldn't absorb their explanations. This was before the conversation with Joan at the Farm. In the usual fashion of our family, I asked the others instead of asking Joan directly why she was angry with me. Like the game of telephone, these sister chains are unreliable, and I was engaged in my own inability to hear. These sister chains make it possible to hide. And I hid. In the indirectness I could come to believe, did come to believe, that Joan was mad because I hadn't told her about Dan. But that was not the case. Here was the case:

Jenny was the one to rip the bandage off. Joan was complaining about the man Mom had living with her as a caretaker of the property, the guy who had been there forever, the guy Mom treated and loved as if he were a son. He'd done something inexcusable and, somehow, I felt that I was, in part, being blamed for it. Once again, I hadn't spoken up when I should have, and the speaking up that I did do hadn't been enough. Joan was angry about that. Mom was still in her right mind and the speaking up had redounded to her, but she had done nothing. Rather she had tried to cover up, and because I was there I became an accomplice. I should have done more, but I didn't understand what more meant. When I was writing my first novel, *Bright Angel Time*, I would read passages to a sister, ask her editorial advice. Once she suggested that, *Tin Drum*–like, I make the narrator a mute. I felt mute. I felt I had no voice with which to speak. I could feel it, the constriction, the words in my head a stew, swirling in there, trapped in there, confusing me. Yet here I was. I was always here, had made my life's work about being here. Here was my Elsewhere. Yet still I had no voice. An incomplete voice. "Have you ever written about it?" Joan had asked. In Joan's moment of indignation about the caretaker, Jenny spoke up about Dan because she couldn't stand to see Joan live in the lie anymore. I wasn't with Joan and Jenny, but I heard about it—and this is how I interpreted it.

It's a family disease, it ripples across generations, burrows in, the secrets like seeds carried in bird droppings, lodging deep in the ground to emerge years later. If our shame silences and we can't speak up for ourselves, how can we possibly speak up for others—for our sisters, our sons, our daughters, our nieces, our nephews, our friends?

SECRETS: AS A YOUNG girl there were so many secrets to keep straight it became easier not to speak at all. We weren't allowed to let Dad know we'd seen Dan when he was dating Mom, or Mom know that we'd seen Yolanda. Waiting for my mother to pick me up from school, I'd been invited into the principal's office. Mom could be very late. I was eight years old. I sat there for a long time. Finally, the principal joined me and started to ask questions about why I had not taken the bus home. I wasn't allowed to take the bus because the bus would drop me at my father's house, my old house on Drake's Corner Road, and it wasn't his allotted, court-mandated time with me. I wasn't allowed to say that because his was the address I used to attend the public school. I wasn't allowed to say I lived in Ringoes or that Dan smoked pot or that my mother was pregnant. There was so much I couldn't say that I said nothing, fearing I'd make a mistake.

I loved Joan very much, but I had also always been jealous of her. My sisters had been able to love her and care for her like older sisters do of the baby; I was jealous of that, too. I wanted them to care for me the way they cared for her. I wanted to be littlest of all. When Joan was a newborn, I dropped her seven times—on her head. I watched her growing up, watched the love that went from Dan to her from her to Dan, ricocheting back and forth, unwavering. Yes, her hero. With my secret released there was no lie between us, no silencing power to rob generosity, to interfere with closeness.

"Love him," Mom had told us, her four McPhee daughters. Did she tell him to love us? Did he love us? Every year I remember his birthday, March 20, 1930. Had I died before him, would he have remembered mine?

I'D LONG SINCE DISCOVERED the endless pockets of garbage in the woods surrounding the house, had hired dumpsters to remove it, but when the workers I had employed in January were clearing rocks from the former bamboo area, they discovered a whole new order of garbage—scraps of sharp metal, shards of glass, shingles and railroad ties, metal poles. I was determined to clean this up, but it slowed down the work of the men, so I put on gloves and worked full-time myself, picking it up and putting it in garbage bins that I placed at the end of the driveway for the garbage man to pick up and haul off. By now, I was on a first-name basis with the garbage man, John. I'd send him pictures of the bins I wanted hauled off, and he'd write back, "I've got you."

What was I doing?

I will tell you what I was doing. All this junk, years and years and years of it, from the tiniest pieces to the biggest pieces, thrown into the woods as if the trees would somehow magically eat it, all of it was haunting me, and I was getting rid of it. This was as an exorcism. I was excising all that was ugly from the past. Piece by piece by piece.

WAS I MAD AT my mother? When she was about four years into her dementia, we discovered that she needed a hip replacement. My sisters and I arranged for this, all of us in New York for the surgery. At a doctor's appointment the nurse attending Mom said to Jenny and me that she could always tell when parents had been good to their children, had loved their children well. "You can see this by how the adult children treat their debilitated parents. You were clearly well-loved; you aren't mean. Some children can be so mean to their parents." Later, as Mom's dementia worsened, I grew increasingly impatient and short-tempered with her, even mean. It's not uncommon for this to happen between dementia patients and their children. Then I'd think of the nurse and how my impatience was getting worse. Had Mom been a good mother? Was I a good child? Had I been the well-loved child the nurse thought she saw in me?

After the surgery one night, at four a.m., my mother called me from the hospital. Even with dementia she could still recite my telephone number. Once, I had answered a call from her and she said, simply, "Who is this? I know this number is important, but who's there?" I told her it was me, Martha—Laura, Sarah, Jenny, Martha, Joan. Martha, your fourth baby. "Come get me," she had said, "I need to get out of here."

That night, four a.m., Mom in the Hospital for Special Surgery, she called my number again, saying that if I didn't get to her immediately, she would never speak to me again. I jumped up, dressed, got in a cab, raced through empty city streets, and was at my mother's side in twenty minutes.

"He's trying to kill me," she said of the night nurse.

Alone at the Farm that late winter of 2021, my family Elsewhere, I would take Mom for walks in the former bamboo grove, bundle her up in boots and her big warm coat, hat, scarf, mittens. I wanted to show her what I'd done, show her my vision for the Sandy Stand. I wanted her to admire my work, be proud of me, grateful. "Martha, what a fabulous job you've done."

Yes, had I been able I would have asked the one essential question that, by its nature, would spawn others. *Had she been awake? What did she know and when?* I wouldn't have allowed her to hide behind the easiness of "Men do that." I would have pressed. I would have asked her to tell me how she justified it, rationalized it. Why did she stay with Dan when she knew? Why did she ask us to love him? What was she afraid of?

"Where would I have gone?" she'd have answered.

Maybe. Maybe that's what she would have said. This story, this relationship with my mother, it's like an object that when held to the light changes to both reveal and hide terrain. She stayed with Dan because she was weak, because she had Joan. She went to work, and she never stopped. She hid behind the work. She turned a blind eye. Look at the sheer number of her negatives in the basement and you can see how she hid. I feel sorry for her, too, because she never got to know herself. She created a bit of a myth for herself and railed against those who didn't see her as kind and good. Look at all I have done, she'd say. In turning a blind eye, she sacrificed us, or at least she did not protect us. But long ago I forgave her, or at least came to understand that we are complex, can hold two very different things at the same time: turn a blind eye, love our children ferociously. She loved us ferociously and wanted everything for us. I am a writer because of her, because she believed in that possibility for me and encouraged me in that direction from a young age even when I was the most unlikely of her children to succeed at a literary career, given that I didn't read, couldn't spell, and was terrible at school. The irony of her blind eye is that, even so, she could see for all of us, deep into the future—where the dreams of the present could become manifest if we believed. She believed for us and that helped us believe. Perhaps her only way out of hiding was through us, her daughters. We were her long horizon.

MY MIDNIGHT READING INCLUDED a piece about trees also suffering plagues, by Gabriel Popkin in the *New York Times*, "Invasive Insects and Diseases Are Killing Our Forests." The news wasn't good. While much attention is focused on wildfires and climate change, invasive species are the greater threat to forest biodiversity and also to the climate itself. Rotting trees killed by pests in U.S. forests release carbon dioxide into the atmosphere on par with the rate released by forest fires. These pest plagues, inflicted by humans through global trade, weakened regulations, and carelessness, are destroying forests while increasing the chances of humans being exposed to more dangerous pathogens. "If we want forests to protect us, we first need to protect them," the article concludes.

HERE'S ANOTHER WAY I can look at my mother and what she may have known and understood: she understood everything. She felt the waterbed slosh. She could see Dan chase my sister, push her fingers back until she said "Uncle." Mom witnessed the fights, the temper, the sadism. In the later stages of her dementia, she was so worried about the babies. She'd ask after the babies all the time, afraid for the babies. She foresaw disaster, death, even. She knew she put her children in harm's way. She did not do this out of cruelty. She is not a cruel person. She did it out of an unnatural, subservient nature toward men. She was raised to be beautiful—not smart. My father fell in love with her because she was beautiful, and smart enough. Dan, too, was drawn to her beauty. Of her intelligence, he often compared her unfavorably to Sally. Sally was smarter. If I wanted Dan to think that I was smart, I can only imagine what my mother desired. And God forbid you made a man feel bad. In her beautiful photography, she did find herself . . . but she never stopped worrying about disasters and death. *Where are the babies?* She knew she put her children in harm's way, and I don't believe she ever forgave herself. *Where are the babies?* She didn't have the strength to act. She knew, and if she found herself at all, she found herself through some of that knowledge, which comes out in her photography, especially when she captures children. Yes, there is joy, but there can also be a veneer of joy overlaying sadness. She didn't mean to hurt anyone. She had no voice. I understand the vise grip of voicelessness, the accommodations made to it, the convoluted bending, turns and twists of subterfuge intended to right the capsized ship of silence. Her voice became her photography.

"Write it all down," she'd say to me as a little girl. She implored me to keep a journal, which I did. She was imploring me to have a voice, to speak.

IN MARCH I WENT to Idaho, the trip that launched this story, crying all the way there as my mind flooded with images of my healthy mother, who had been gone to me for so long. I was afraid that once gone, I would never want to return. Out of sight, out of mind. Perhaps my own life could take over—my son, my husband, the novel I was working on. "It will eat you alive," Laura had said of the Farm. It was a Venus flytrap, a plant that fascinated me as a kid. Could a plant really eat a human? Had the Farm swallowed me whole?

But I returned to New Jersey. My sisters were still unable to travel, in their various lockdown Elsewheres. Dayana needed relief. "What would happen if you simply didn't return?" a friend asked.

The truth, a truth, was—I loved being at the Farm. It was becoming clear that by September 2021, with vaccinations readily available for most, schools would be in person. There would be a natural endpoint to my time in New Jersey. I would return to my apartment and my job. I would be in the classroom again. My sisters would be able to travel more easily, and they'd be able to help relieve Dayana. There are five of us sisters; I imagined we could take turns. There was time to figure it out. In any case, I would need to leave when school started up again six months from now. In the meantime, I'd continue living at the Farm.

IN APRIL, I RECEIVED an email letting me know that I could pick up the saplings. I felt both excited and daunted. I drove to the nature center in Washington Crossing State Park, where a man from the sapling nursery awaited customers coming for their orders. Around a series of picnic tables were dozens upon dozens of brown bags with twigs poking from them—some more abundant than others, all of them little sticks of hope.

I took my bundle home and went directly to the paddock. I'd watched Duke's video a few times. He literally made a divot in the dirt and popped the saplings in the ground. I took mine from their brown bag. The twigs, very dead seeming, had intricate, full root systems. I had fifty. As it turns out, I wasn't able to just pop them in the ground. I dug deep holes and filled each one with water, then carefully with dirt, making certain the roots were submerged. I didn't always get the depth right and would have to redo the effort. By the end of the day, all the saplings were planted, ten tidy rows, five saplings per row. For days, my hands and my hips ached.

The earth was rich from all the years of animal droppings. Over by the fence, just a few feet from the trees, stood a faucet.

B ack in September 2020, no end in sight for the pandemic, realizing I'd be staying in New Jersey much longer than I had
imagined, I took all the ancestors off the walls in Grammy's room. I
put them in Mom's bedroom closet. I moved out the ugly, big heavy
wooden dresser that had been in my grandmother's bedroom in her
home in Maine when I was a child. In one of the small top drawers
of the highboy she had kept her smelling salts and would ask us, her
granddaughters, to get them for her from time to time when she was
feeling faint. "I'm just an old threadbare mule," she'd say, clutching
at her chest. Her home was called Last Morrow; she had an active,
maudlin sense of drama.

I moved the ancestors. I moved the highboy. I moved the long
opera coats and the beaver fur stiff with dry rot, and I started referring to the room as *my room* . . . or at least I stopped referring to it as
Grammy's room. She had been dead twenty-five years. On the wall
against which the dresser had stood, I hung a Haitian painting de-
picting a voodoo ceremony that involved women with weirdly long
arms washing something in vessels beneath an abstract tree with little doors and an abstract crown shading the women from a night sky.

I felt an immediate sense of lightness. It was a relief to have my great-grandmother Glenna's eyes, Grammy's eyes, my uncle's eyes, and so many other eyes, including my own as a child, off of me. In the beginning of the pandemic, when my mother came into the room, she would recognize her brother and ask about him. "That's my brother. Where is he? Where has he gone?" Sometimes she would ask me if he was dead. The story of her brother lived fully in my memory, but no longer in hers. He had died of a stroke, but they'd been estranged, hadn't spoken in years—some form of unforgivable betrayal, the kind that happens in families. But she didn't remember all that. What she recalled was that he was her brother, her handsome brother, and she wanted him. In a way that is common with dementia patients, she often had an immediate and urgent desire to see him from which she could not be distracted or cajoled. But that, too, passed, and she soon no longer asked after him, or recognized him in the photograph.

I took all but three pictures down, leaving my mother as a girl, her face framed in sausage curls; my mother as a bride; myself as a girl, just after my mother cut my hair. I'd had long hair and for some reason she had cut it. My father had been so furious he grabbed our long-haired orange cat, named Bingham for Dad's *New Yorker* editor, and he shaved it—or so the story goes. I do love family stories, how they tumble down the years. The cat-shaving had to be an exaggeration, but there it was. How in the world do you shave a cat? When I was born my mother was covered in poison ivy, from head to toe, contracted while gardening. She handed me to Dad and told him to name me. She was too uncomfortable to be bothered. He named me

Martha, which became "He named you for an old girlfriend." And we still, all of us, say that to this day, even as Dad denies it.

Getting rid of the ancestors, I understood finally Katherine Anne Porter's ending to "Old Mortality," the weight and oppression of the past. "I can't live in their world any longer, she told herself, listening to the voices back of her. Let them tell their stories to each other. Let them go explaining how things happened. I don't care. At least I can know the truth about what happens to me . . ."

Is this what Elsewhere meant?

OVER THE YEARS, MY sisters and I would speculate about what we would do with the Farm. One of the notions we had fun with, in a serious moment of fantasy, was that we could (not would) all grow old together at the Farm. Never mind that we didn't always get on, certainly not when we were all together. We were better in pairs, but we all seemed to laugh mightily, anyway, at the darkly comic thought of us growing old and losing our minds together at the Farm-as-retirement-home. We had architectural fantasies for how we'd reconfigure the house so that we each had a room we'd enjoy as our own. We'd employ the cottages, build up and reconstruct the space that had been the indoor pool so that it became a gorgeous room with big windows overlooking the forest, those enormous windows with steel divides—a fireplace.

We'd read an article about friends who created their own retirement community plan, bought a house together in which to grow old. We sent it around to each other. "See?" We were on to something. There was an article about medical-pods-on-wheels that you parked in your yard like an Airstream but that had all the necessary technology and medical equipment to care for the aging. "See?" We could each have our own medical pod at Omega Farm. Maybe that would be our Omega Point.

I never wanted to let go; I had liked the fantasy—a place in the future where we could all be returned to an unburdened past.

I planted the sugar maples in the paddock and across the summer they grew. The twigs sprouted; a few lost their leaves and seemed to be dead, only to sprout anew. Rabbits gnawed away at some. We put up protective fencing. The rains were heavy, storms coming in at global-warming strength and speed. Tornado warnings came across alert systems on our phones regularly. Wet and sultry, weeds grew like I had never seen weeds grow before. I weeded around the trees until my hands and hips ached, only to need to repeat the following week. By August I'd lost six saplings. But each morning, the skies dark and hazy from forest fires in the west, I'd water the saplings that remained. I'd watch them bob and sway and glisten in the sprinkler's mist. I would not fail.

In the gardens around the house, I dug up some oak saplings, planted them in pots and raised them in the paddock as well. All in all, I still had forty-five trees. We watered them, fertilized them lightly once a month as Duke instructed in his video. Along the way, I noted a few things I'd do differently—more oak (they're slower to grow, but they last longer), more shade (especially if I continue working with maples), more space, more initial weeding of the paddock.

Daily, I'd walk around the former bamboo forest looking for renegade shoots. Perimeter check, I'd call this exercise, the pick mattock slung over my shoulder. Over the spring and summer months I found just five.

ENDINGS DON'T ALWAYS COME with the precision of a guillotine, especially an ending like this one, involving a pandemic that wasn't ending neatly, a mother whose dying was steady if slow, a deep love of a place tethered to ghosts and the past.

WHEN MY MOTHER WAS first diagnosed with dementia, Sarah and I slipped into a fast denial. We'd tell each other that it wasn't so bad, describe for each other all the things that Mom could remember and do. Laura hired an expert who assessed Mom and told her what to expect about Mom's decline, made suggestions for safety features we should install at the Farm. Joan moved to California for a job, had a daughter and then twins with her wife. Mom visited her. She visited Mom. But Joan was busy. Joan was the first for Mom to forget. Last born, first forgotten.

At a Jamaican Christmas dinner at the home of Joan's sister-in-law, all their family collected around the table, all of them Black except for Mom and Joan, Mom looked around the table and then to Joan and asked, "How do I know you?"

"I am your daughter," Joan answered, tears immediately welling in her eyes.

"Really?"

"Really."

"Well, then I want to know all about you," Mom said.

One by one she forgot us all. Jenny wrote a beautiful essay about Mom's dementia for the *New York Times*.

Laura was convinced that Mom's dementia was caused by Lyme disease, that if she had the proper antibiotics her memory would return. Sometimes I would lie in bed late at night and picture that her memory had been restored because the doctors had somehow removed the plaque in her brain, the way a dental hygienist scrapes plaque from your teeth with a special sharp instrument like a scalpel.

The sisters and I could spend long stretches debating which was better to have: dementia or Alzheimer's, somehow forgetting that this was not a game of Would You Rather. It seemed somewhere we decided dementia was better and that Mom only had dementia.

When our stepfather lay dying of pancreatic cancer, we all did the same thing. We looked for cutting-edge treatments, studies, alternative remedies. In the last days of his life, he drank awful concoctions of blended fruit and a powder made from shark cartilage and bovine something or other.

Articles appear all the time about progress in the search for the cure for dementia, different drugs, different therapies. We would send them around to each other, bursts of hope flying across the internet to land in our inboxes. Light therapy—Sarah read about it, found a doctor at Emory who specialized in the research.

And so it went.

Then one day we all found ourselves in a pandemic and I ended up with my family at the Farm. As millions of people around the world died, as we were all locked in place, my sisters, of course, couldn't visit. I made the best of it with my kids and my husband, the lovely, beautiful caregiver with her striking name: Dayana—pronounced *Day Shana*—long *a*. Diana in English. Dayana had left Colombia and planned never to return. After nine months, she was able to bring her son. We made arrangements so that he would have a lovely room, my former room in the basement. For a while, we were a family, a pandemic family made of circumstance. Dayana enrolled Juanpa in the local school—the same one Joan had attended as a child. Dayana secured medical insurance for Juanpa and herself. She applied for a driver's license. She used our car to go on excursions with her son. I helped make this possible and the effort made me happy. By taking care of Dayana and Juanpa I was also taking care of Mom. In the evenings we ate those dinners together, laughing, enjoying stories, teaching each other bits of English and Spanish. Dayana treated my mother with generous love that made Mom feel safe and attended to. She played catch with Mom, walked with her, bathed her, cut her nails, her hair, cleaned her, dressed her stylishly with a spritz of perfume, an elegant necklace. She massaged Mom. She gave Mom projects. Dayana also worked hard on herself when Mom slept, which she did until noon each day. Dayana took courses to become a life coach for individuals and for corporations. She intended to volunteer in prisons, for prisoner rehabilitation. I was impressed by her, disciplined, motivated. Her son was disciplined and motivated too. They took a vacation, traveling to Boston so that he could see Harvard, and he decided he would do whatever it took to get there. He was twelve years old.

I lived in fear of her leaving, that rural New Jersey would soon be too isolating. Her mother lived in Queens, had recently moved into a bigger apartment. As I have mentioned, fear can take possession of me. If Dayana left, I imagined it would be impossible to replace her, especially during a global pandemic. The burden of caring for Mom would fall entirely to me and I wouldn't be able to do it. This entire fragile enterprise of keeping Mom at home would come crashing down if Dayana left. So I did what Mom had always done. I gave and then I gave some more. If I only gave enough, Dayana would never leave. As a child I was diagnosed as a slow learner by a learning specialist in New York City. The doctor's name was Katrina de Hirsch, famous, a pioneer in the study of learning disabilities in children. Dad sent me to her because of how poorly I did in school. There had to be something wrong and there was: I was a slow learner.

Caregiving of any sort is no easy task. Incontinence was now permanent. Increasingly, in the evenings, sundowning set in. Mom became defiant, wanted to leave, get out of here, get home. Sometimes she'd literally run away, and it would take Dayana, her son, and me to coax Mom back inside. On a walk one day, she fled from Dayana, ending up in the neighbor's living room, the old Vieceli home, owned now by the man who had generously plowed our driveway. Mom pleaded with him to save her. Dayana managed to persuade Mom to leave the neighbor's house. Later, he called me to let me know what happened, to ask if all was all right. Just as often as there are hopeful articles about possible cures, there are others about the toll caregiving takes on the caregiver, especially the children of the patient, the spouse. Watching my mother die inch by inch, even with help, was far more stressful than I allowed. I hid the stress behind the beauty of the dahlias and the garden, behind the colorful eggs I collected each morning and afternoon, behind the rooster who liked to attack me each time I collected those beautiful eggs, behind the dogs and the evening walks with the sunset splayed out against the vast sky, behind the home improvement projects, the bamboo and the septic, my trees, the forest.

In the evenings sometimes, when Mom became particularly anxious, I'd turn on Frank Sinatra to calm her down. Or Doris Day singing "Que Sera, Sera." "Hey, Alexa," I'd say to the little round robot listening to our world, and soon came Doris Day's tender voice, pulling Mom from her chair.

When I was just a little girl
I asked my mother, what will I be

Mom's face would light up with the past. She'd start to dance, and I would dance with her, the two of us in a deep embrace, swirling around the kitchen, her head tucked into my shoulder. I could feel her happiness against my own. This was why I was here, why I stayed. Sometimes I'd play the song a few times.

IF CARETAKING MOM WAS taking its toll on me, it was also taking its toll on Dayana. She did not tell me that it was, but I could feel it—a fatigue. I could also brush it aside, believe it was my fear and not her reality. She had been with us fifteen months at this point, coming from Colombia at the end of January just before the pandemic shut down the world. About three months into the job, she thanked me, told me she had been in deep debt and hadn't known how she would ever get out of it. This job had helped her pay off her last bill. She had tears in her eyes. This had made me happy. But time had passed, and she had made a couple missteps and was back in debt. I wanted to help her fix it. Mom-like, I wanted to find the solution that solved everything. I wanted us to be one big happy family. I wanted to be good and do and help, in the process make being at the Farm a good thing for Dayana, a place where she could raise her son and build her coaching business while taking care of Mom. I thought of her as a daughter, a sister, rarely as an employee. I thought if I could take care of everything she would never leave and if she never left Mom would be okay, indefinitely, permanently all right.

*　*　*

HERE IS WHERE I became ugly.

The pandemic, that summer of 2021, was surging in parts of the country, especially where people showed a disinclination to get vaccinated or wear masks. Who is the three-headed beast from mythology? Cerberus, monstrous watchdog of the underworld. The virus was lashing out again with the Delta variant, to be followed soon by Omicron, scaring everyone all over again, creating a new fatigue. Masks off, masks on. Lines and lines and longer lines for tests at COVID testing sites. Those little circles on the ground, instructing us to keep our distance, dirty from so much use. It seemed everyone was sick.

Across the pandemic my children grew up, my parents grew older. Weekly I delivered groceries to my father. Sometimes I'd make a lasagna or scones or loaves of whole wheat bread. I'd bring produce from the garden, always the beautiful, colorful eggs. I'd leave the bags outside their front door and wave to them standing at the window, just as so many others were doing across the world.

After we'd both had the first dose of the vaccination, I went inside. My stepmother grabbed ahold of me and kissed me, hugged me for a long time. We all started crying. Her arms around me, familiar and unfamiliar, had been relegated to a memory—something we all once did and might never do again. My father and I spoke endlessly on the phone. He loved knowing that I was in New Jersey, just ten minutes away should something go wrong. He took pleasure in all my stories about the garden and the chickens, the rooster's attacks, the bamboo.

Under the bam
Under the boo
Under the bamboo tree

He recited the poem to me.

But when we came out of hiding, when our masks came off and we could hug and kiss again, spend time together again in the same room, I could see how he and Yolanda had aged. He'd become older. Not surprising at ninety, but somehow startling all the same. He was unsteady on his feet, his balance compromised by peripheral neuropathy, his vision compromised by glaucoma. *Scumble* was the word he used to describe what it was like to see through his eyes: as if through a thin, opaque coat of paint or layer of shading applied to give a softer or duller effect—taken directly from the dictionary. There are, Dad told me in the way he loves to do, delighting in facts and knowledge, eleven words in the English language that end in "umble." When he would ask his students to name them, they would get ten, always missing *scumble*.

He was still as sharp as ever, still precise, still working, still writing, still riding his bike ten miles every other day.

My stepmother: two minor strokes that predated the pandemic had set off her own dementia and she had begun to withdraw into herself. She spent a good deal of the day sleeping.

Back at home, my daughter had turned from girl to woman—wise and ambitious, patient with the slow progress of return to normal.

She'd taken a course on managing emotions and had learned a calm, meditative peace that was inspiring to witness.

My son was breaking away, finding us, his parents, insufferable, the Farm unbearable. Disappointments stacked up for him, one after the next, and through those months there was a loss of the self that he was fighting to find, and it was messy. The pandemic had taken its toll on kids everywhere.

That toll revealed itself in the summer of 2021, for Jasper, for me, perhaps for us all. We'd been in New Jersey for a year and three months. It was easy to forget that Jasper was a child, that when you're seventeen a year is a long time. It all started adding up— Jasper's refusal to even visit the Farm, juggling him and the reality of Mom, missing Mark, who stayed in New York most of the time with Jasper, Mom's slow death, the daily demands I'd taken on and to which I had given myself completely, solving and fixing and making it all better, enduring, making the best of things. *Residual omnipotence* is what we jokingly called it, this attribute. It never works. All the giving of *The Giving Tree* builds up and I explode: one of my nicknames in childhood was Martilla the Hun. Somewhere I never learned to manage my limits, or never even learned the idea of limits. This was something the trees were teaching me, but I was slow to learn. *Manage better*, my daughter says. *Don't give so much*, my son says. When I come apart, the episodes come on like violent storms. Example: when, at the beginning of the pandemic, I disappeared into the night, crying in my car at the gas station. I'm returned to an out-of-control child who has no power over her world, a kid who can't stand the chaos, who wants out, and there is no way to get there, no exit.

When we went to Haiti, Dan and Mom organized a day-long outing to Bassin Bleu, waterfalls in the hills above Jacmel. The entire lot of us were to hike into the forest to what promised to be a spectacular spot, a once-in-a-lifetime opportunity to see natural beauty. The morning of the excursion, I pretended to be sick with whatever the disease was that foreigners all got in Haiti—the grippe. I lay in bed complaining of a headache, said I couldn't go, begged them to leave me behind. They did. For the entire hot hot day, I was alone in the house, the sounds and smells of the town drifting up to me from the street. I thought of the family all together, seeing the beauty; I felt utterly alone. I wanted to be alone, but I didn't know what to do with myself. I wished I'd been able to go. I was mad at myself for missing out, for pretending to be sick, but also relieved to have time all to myself and to be in charge of it even if I did nothing. I dwelled in the tension between my solitude and my eagerness for their return.

BY THE SUMMER OF 2021 we were all vaccinated. Vaccinated, the sisters returned individually, one by one, to see Mom. I was excited to see them, to show off all that I had accomplished—the bamboo forest now an emerald lawn, my maple trees growing in the paddock, the ambition for the understory in the Sandy Stand. My chickens and their eggs. I even wanted to show them the mess the logger had made in Stand 1. The sisters had comments, made observations, expressed gratitude for the improvements, for my physical presence at the Farm and the comfort it gave to Mom to have a daughter with her. But there was also this:

Late evening with one sister. A couple of glasses of wine were involved—an essential service. Seated on the bed in "Grammy's room" (dead twenty-five years), no longer "Grammy's room." My clothes in the closet, a lot of my clothes, winter and summer, filling the closet. My creams and vitamins, my Q-tips, my jewelry, on the vanity. My work and papers and checkbook on the desk. My shoes on the floor. Mark's clothes in the other closet. His notebooks and books on the bedside table. Copies of the novel I'd recently published and peddled, standing, six of them, on a shelf above the sliding glass door—the only title up there.

Across the hall, my daughter had made a room for herself in the room we referred to as the "loft" room. Growing up my stepbrothers, Hy and Tony, had shared it. But across the pandemic, Livia had made it hers—strung up fairy lights, made a collage of snapshots on one of the walls as kids do in their dorm rooms, taken down a Haitian painting or two. Her clothes spilled from the closet. Her things covered many surfaces. On the door she had pinned a beautiful little painting that said "Livia's Room." It had been given to her by the RA of her dormitory at college. It had stars and trees, her name in silver script. She had placed it on the door, staking her claim to the room. She had lived in this room during lockdown, had returned to it during that first Thanksgiving and Christmas of the pandemic when her college was remote for two months, had returned again for the summer of 2021 because the summer internship she had (writing articles on dementia for a psychology department newsletter) was remote. Having Livia in New Jersey helped me in taking care of Mom, so I wasn't doing the job alone when Dayana took her days off and her vacation. Livia wasn't here. I was alone with my sister, seated on a bed I had bought for the room because the one that had been here was old and uncomfortable. I'd bought new sheets, a down comforter, pillows, lamp shades, had had the room painted. I had done the same with the loft room, new bed and all the rest. We had been here for 1.4 years, still counting. We had made ourselves at home.

This one sister and I were chatting pleasantly when I referred to "Livia's room." My sister turned to me with a sudden violence in her eyes and snapped, "That is not Livia's room. You make a mistake here. This is not your room. This is not your house. You do not own this house."

I looked at her. I knew what was coming. Her storms could come on equal to mine. I was exhausted. I sighed and asked if she really wanted to do this. I looked at her, holding her with my eyes.

"You're making a serious mistake," she said. I had been here living in the house, a good thing for all of us, but with this sister's visit, with the reality of my stuff all over the house, all over the room, Livia's name on the bedroom door, it felt like we were thieves, my family and I, like I was stealing the house, the house an object I could walk off with. She started spewing stuff. I tried to remain calm. I know how these things go, knew this was irrational, knew how the irrational takes hold, how fear slips in, how childhood returns to haunt. The Farm has a hold on us. I know that. Can feel that. None of us is immune. And we had been here before, other arguments, different combinations of sister—but none of us was immune. The storm rises in us until it takes over completely and we cannot see the other, the love gets clobbered out. Eventually the storm passes.

But I engaged.

"I've been here for a while," I said. "This is the room I've been staying in. That is the room Livia has been staying in. Having Livia here makes it possible for me to be here." Livia was on a much-needed vacation with her boyfriend, returning in the morning. The job of caring for Mom was no longer a job for one person. Mom could no longer do anything for herself. I helped Dayana; Livia helped me.

My sister stood up and went to Livia's door and took down the hand-painted sign with her name in the intricate silver script.

I think I said something about being here for Mom. Defensively I started listing the things that I had done. "That was your choice," my sister snapped. "You made that decision. No one forced you to do this. The choice was yours. You wanted to escape the pandemic." A spray of language and my year with my mother at the Farm reduced in an instant to nothing but a simple, self-serving choice. I loved this sister. I love her very much, admire her, look up to her, wanted to be like her as a child, a younger woman, could still see her placing a flower in a little vase to adorn the breakfast tray we brought to our mother in bed after Dad left. I wanted her to see me. I wanted us to be far away from here, thick in a relationship that had nothing to do with the past, with this present of caring for Mom.

Instead, I snapped, grabbed my suitcase from the closet and shoved some of my things into it. "I'm leaving. I don't need to be here. I have a husband and son in New York. I have a home and I'm going to it now." I desperately wanted to be at my home with my husband, my family. Home blossomed in me like a surprise. I had a home. Yes, this wasn't my home, my home was in New York City, and I could go there right now. My sister was to be here several days. She could see what it was like taking care of Mom by herself. Dayana and Juanpa were away, visiting her mother. I pushed past my sister as she tried to block the door. "I'm going home. You figure it out without me."

"Please don't leave," she said, calming herself down quite suddenly. Perhaps she was seeing me, but it was too late. She'd ignited me. She'd insulted me. She had been cruel—the way we can think it is all right to be with one another. She looked at me, realizing that she'd gone too far and that she'd need to work hard to fix this. But I didn't care. I hated her—the way it happens, the way we can feel, a switch.

I lugged my things swiftly to the car, loaded it, and got in. It was raining hard, and it was late, very dark. I started the engine and put the car in reverse. I could do this. I was flooded with a sense of freedom. I didn't need to be here anymore. I could go home. I had a home. This wasn't my home. Just then my sister jumped into the passenger seat. "I'm not getting out," she said. "If you go, you're taking me with you."

"Get out," I screamed. "You're an awful person," I screamed. I started backing up. She pressed the Park button. The car jolted to a stop. I was blind with fury, spitting out every experience I'd shared and endured with Mom, but I knew as it was flooding out that I didn't want to leave, that I wanted to be here with her, my sister, that I wanted this storm to pass as they always do. Tomorrow it would be sunny, and we'd find a project to work on together and we'd love each other again, delight in each other again, dream together as we had so many times before about how we could make this all better and meaningful, and we'd do this by pulling up some weeds and imagining more ways to fix all that needed fixing. I understood that the rage was childhood rearing its head, and that neither one of us would ever let the other go. It was a rage of powerlessness—mine, hers. We were prisoners, afraid, terrified, and out it all came as it had before, as it would again. I knew in the midst of my wild windstorm that I would not leave, but I let her plead and beg and urge and apologize and beg some more for me to stay, for me to forgive her.

Trauma is a word that none of us likes to use, feels qualified to use. We don't allow ourselves to think of ourselves as having been traumatized in childhood. Growing up we were supposed to normalize and rationalize: Dan was playful; we were an adventurous family; we went on great trips, were taught the importance of travel when our friends were returning to the same shacks on Fire Island year after year. But rage needs to escape and this, it seems, is how it escaped from us, sideways yet aimed at each other—our relationships again another casualty of our past.

Eventually the anger blew out. I lugged my suitcase inside. She asked if we could just pretend the fight never happened.

Even so, this episode didn't put an end to the comments from some of the sisters, who were concerned, it seemed, that I might never leave. My presence was no longer a good thing. I had become, I felt, like another unwanted stranger who came for a weekend and stayed and stayed and stayed. Your childhood home has a firm grip. When the sisters visited the Farm, they too would work overtime to fix things that needed fixing. Childhood is an onrushing, ever-present nightmare inside a musty house with a dying mother none of us wants to let go of. We all want something from the past.

ONE MORNING SHORTLY AFTER the blowup, Dayana and Juanpa still away, my mother woke earlier than usual and escaped, walked out the front door and got into the car parked near the upper cottage. The car belonged to Sarah's boyfriend—Sarah of the upper cottage. Mom took off her dirty diaper, peed. She then took off her clothes until she was naked. On the floor of the car, she found a pair of sneakers belonging to the boyfriend. She put them on. Sarah found her and called me. It took my sister, Livia, and me to get Mom back inside and cleaned up. This wasn't the first time; it wouldn't be the last.

"Forgive me," my sister said again. "I know how much you've done." Funny thing, how her comment soaked into me, how I absorbed it fully, loving her even more for it.

* * *

THAT SUMMER, SUMMER 2021, September looming, my year in New
Jersey sliding to the finish line, teaching about to start again in person: taking a walk at dusk with our dogs as Mark, Livia, and I like
to do, we always admire the view, the sinking sun splashing the sky
with crazy beauty. This, the Farm, is as beautiful as anywhere we've
ever been.

I have two dogs, Gigi and Luna; my mother has one, Leo. We love
these dogs, consider Leo to be ours as well. But they are loud. Gigi
barks at anything that comes up the driveway. She barks at squirrels
and birds. The foxes drive her wild. She howls at the fire station siren
that sounds at noon every day in Ringoes. Her howl is like a wolf's.
Luna is a pandemic puppy, a rescue from the streets of Tennessee,
the sweetest, smartest dog, full of play and puppy stuff, so eager to
please, a mix of Lab and German shepherd—or so we were told. Her
veterinarian thinks Luna has a healthy dose of short-haired Afghan
in her genetic makeup. She's fast as a greyhound. She barks at the
cats, catches rabbits, mice, and birds and brings them to us as little
presents. Leo, he's an old man, watches the world, his butt on the
deck, his front legs on the top step leading down to the lawn. When
Gigi barks she sets off Luna, then Leo.

I'm getting to the ugly.

Dayana could sit with Mom for hours, patiently letting Mom
braid her hair. Dayana was not an expert in the field of eldercare,
let alone dementia. She was an ambitious woman, working hard to
make a career in a field that interested her. While Mom slept and

while her son was at school, Dayana worked hard to become certified in life coaching by taking an online course. Once that was complete, she set up shop with a fancy website, found a few clients. She inspired us all to work harder. In the summer of 2021, with the sisters returning, with more visitors appearing, with my own messes resulting from Jasper's refusal to return to the Farm, with the new puppy, Dayana told me she needed more order. She asked if she could make some changes. She wanted to eat her main meal of the day at lunchtime. She believed it would be better for Mom. She wanted the meals to be just with her, Juanpa, and Mom. She didn't want me to cook for her. There were other things, jobs she would no longer do, more days off, nothing unreasonable. I'm not sure what was in her heart at this time, but it seemed she needed clearer boundaries, that the communal meals such as they were no longer worked for her. It seemed she needed to better control her environment. As summer moved along, every day there was a new concern. I tried to accommodate. Often, there was a favor, some problem that I tried to solve. A problem with her bank and a loan, editing of her website so the English was correct. The fear grew, the terror of her leaving, of being alone at the Farm with my mother. I kept trying to fix the situation, kept offering more, said yes to the requests, sought ways to help. I began to feel like a hamster in a wheel, like I couldn't move fast enough to keep it all spinning, but fear kept me running faster and faster and faster. This situation worked for all of us, most of all my mother, as long as Dayana was there. Finding eldercare help is extremely hard and Mom's illness had progressed.

The ugly.

Jasper was in New York City, alone at our apartment—Mark in New Jersey for a few days to help with the trees and the chickens, the garden and the garbage (a job that became ours across the pandemic, getting the tenants' garbage and recycling to the foot of the driveway on schedule with pickup), to help me and Livia with Mom. But it wasn't a smart thing for us to do, leave a seventeen-year-old unattended. Jasper made some choices that were alarming—staying out too late, partying too much, other things: nothing that Mark or I hadn't done when we were his age, we imagined, but still, it kept us up all night on more than one occasion. Remember, I am prone to fear. On the last of these occasions, we didn't sleep at all and in the morning the situation escalated. Something was wrong, very wrong, though we didn't know what. The not-knowing terrified me. We packed fast, threw our stuff in the car—Livia, Mark, and I. The plan was to get Jasper and come back. We had to get him out of the city. I had been making mistakes left and right.

As we rushed to get out the door, I asked Dayana if she could watch Gigi and Luna for the twelve hours it would take us, possibly twenty-four. I had paid Juanpa on other occasions to watch the dogs. The request felt reasonable, though I knew the dogs could be a handful and she had told me that the barking gave her headaches. I was desperate and I thought that as a mother, she'd understand, so I asked.

She said no. She repeated that the barking gave her a headache. When we weren't there, Luna peed inside the house. I was desperately worried about Jasper. I looked at her, astonished. I wanted someone to help me. I needed help. I felt consumed. She was definitive. I snapped: "Never ask me again for any help or favors," I said, looking at her the way my sister had looked at me on that rainy fight night. I could feel it on my face, a hatred—for her refusal, for the lack of help, for the pandemic, for my fatigue, for my dying mother, for Jasper's troubles. This rage in me, this anger, tethered, as it was, all the way with one long thread to my child self, to wanting to be protected and taken care of, or even just heard. She burst into tears. I apologized immediately. I pleaded forgiveness, swelling with the shame I know so well, but I had blown up with her, and I couldn't take it back.

Perhaps Dayana could see what I had seen in my sister's face when she sat on the bed and told me that I did not own the Farm, a besetting, belligerent unleashing of anger that runs deep in our family. I knew what my sister had felt: some old wrath at powerlessness rearing its ugly snake head, coming forth from the distant past. Dayana, I imagined, saw this directed at her, and her reaction, naturally, was one of self-protection and also protection for her son. She was an employee, but I had grown close, had blurred the boundaries as my mother always liked to do. Dayana was not my sister, after all. She was an employee, employed by my family to care for our mother. We were paying her to be there. She had been trying to define the boundary of employer and employee by eating separately, and somewhere I hadn't liked that clarity. Somewhere it threatened me, made me feel off-balance, perhaps out of control, that my efforts weren't enough to fix the problem. I wanted to fix the problem, all problems, even problems I didn't yet know were problems. I wanted to stop time. The Farm is haunted. No, the Farm is not haunted. We are haunted.

With Dayana in the dining room, as I tried frantically to walk back my bitter comment, to tame my eyes, dread rushed over me—an enormous feeling of failure about My Year in New Jersey, all of it culminating in this hideous moment and I could see the future, clear as day, how it would so painfully unfold. And just then I collapsed, falling to the floor.

A FEW MONTHS EARLIER, in the late winter, two mothers of friends of Jasper's came to visit me. We took a hike through the winter forest. I showed them what I'd been working on—the invasives, the need for management hunters, the issue with the understory. As they were leaving, they noted that they'd both thought about doing what I'd done—returning home and, by some means, somehow, correcting the past. "Even if you can't do it, for whatever reason, it's something we're all thinking about. Can one go home again? What does that look like? What does that mean? You did it," one of my friends said. I was old enough to know that sometimes you just accept a compliment. Yes, I smiled. I had done it.

But I felt like Eurydice, almost out of the underworld; would I make it? I could see the light and it seemed very beautiful indeed.

MARK PICKED ME UP from the floor and got me to the car. I confess; I hoped that fainting would make Dayana see me, see how stressed I was, that I deserved help. What she saw was something else, I imagine, something that terrified her for herself and her son. It was all too much. If she had become increasingly remote, increasingly demanding, I'd become increasingly anxious—that feeling of trying to hold on to water slipping through your fingers. I was so anxious in fact that I needed to take Xanax to help me sleep. Even the small amount I took at night had the weird effect of making me more anxious during the day.

"Did you ever consider," a friend asked, "that you and Dayana were burned out? Most caregivers of dementia patients last seven months. That's the average. You and Dayana did this nonstop for a year and a half."

I had fainted before, the fainting, a vasovagal syncope, my body overreacting to stress. We went back to New York, back to Jasper, bringing the dogs. Jasper was in bed. I lay down next to him. He started crying. He told me all that was troubling him and what had happened the night before. Children everywhere were struggling from the effects of the pandemic. We spoke for hours in his room. He was wise, honest, scared. Toward the end, he said, "It's not natural to return to your childhood home. You grow up and do your own thing. You don't go back."

WHILE I WAS IN New York with Jasper, Dayana gave notice effective immediately. When I returned, all of Dayana's and Juanpa's belongings had been packed and moved. She left behind only two pairs of shoes and two furry blankets that I had given her as presents. I would discover them in the room that had been Dayana's. I sat on her bed, head in hands, sad and sorry for the mess and pain I had caused. My mother's room was next to Dayana's, and Mom was in there, in her bed, oblivious. I was being sucked down a drain into the scary void of the unknown.

"You're not alone. I'm here. Livia and Jasper are here," Mark said, and then he kissed me.

I had a dream in which I am alone in the house at the Farm, a girl again, home from school pretending to be sick. The walls rise around me, higher and higher, until I am very small, dwarfed by the house. Alone.

For what felt like a long time my sisters would not speak to me.

WHEN WE FIRST MOVED to the Farm, I remember worrying that I would not know the way back to Drake's Corner Road. The route was ten miles long with many twists and turns. I studied each turn, memorizing everything, imprinting the route on my mind, indelibly, so that I would never forget the way home.

I BECAME CONSUMED WITH guilt, that tendency I have toward guilt, toward wallowing in it, toward taking it on fully and completely. My act had caused the caregiver to quit. My act had left my mother vulnerable. My act had made my sisters vanish. "She made this mess, she'll need to clean it up," I imagined them saying to one another, perhaps on a sister call that didn't include me. And they'd have been right. I made this mess; it was mine to clean up.

For a long time I felt I needed to explain myself, get into the details, the circumstances, live in the weeds. But I came to see that the details aren't important. Dayana left. I didn't hear from my sisters. They, too, were processing all of this, grief—our dying mother, the end of the past with our narrowing futures. Without a clear perspective, a good perch from which to look back, I sank into a depression that was as bad as any depression I've ever had—and I've had a few. But the depression didn't have to do with Dayana or my sisters. They were all trying their best in this situation with my mother that was harder than any of us could have imagined. Rather, the depression had to do with me, with my relationship to myself. My life's work has been Sisyphean in that I've tried all these years to put my broken family back together again. To save it, patch it, fix it—through fiction, through love, through time, through effort, through Chicken Kiev and cooking for a table of ten, by returning to the Farm during the pandemic, by caring for my mother, by shopping for my father, by selling negatives, by removing the bamboo, by renting dumpsters for all the junk with money I didn't have, from the small gestures to the large deeds, by growing trees and learning about forest restoration, by caring for Dayana and her son, by raising chickens and growing a garden. The depression dwelled in the sinkhole of all my efforts and my reckoning with the fact that I was able to fix nothing. It isn't possible to fix this family. It was broken and reimagined a long time ago. Fixing it was never my job. It was never asked of me, and no one wanted me to take on this impossible task—for me or for them. The only thing I needed to fix was myself. Simple revelation. Obvious revelation. Even so, it eluded me, as the simplest things right in front of us often can.

THE WORLD CONTAINS INTERCONNECTED and layered planes of experience—ecologies that seem separate but aren't. There is the pandemic plane; the financial plane, the wealth gap; the political plane, democracy fighting against authoritarianism, a woman's right to choose; the racial reckoning plane; the global-warming plane. The other day I read about the slowing down of the current in the Atlantic Ocean, a weakening of what is called the Atlantic Meridional Overturning Circulation—a system that brings warm, salty water from the tropics to northern Europe and sends colder water south on the ocean floor. If the AMOC stops functioning the entire weather system shifts—extreme cold, extreme heat, more monsoons, further rising sea levels. And if the AMOC does come to a stop, it might not be possible to restart. Maybe the biggest and most problematic plane of all is the plane of forgetting: each generation awakening to its own peculiar set of challenges, striving to address them, some trying to leave a record—a cave painting on a wall, or a trail of breadcrumbs. But unless we all commit ourselves to the discipline of memory and history, a commitment that often seems impractical, that doesn't pay the rent, the breadcrumbs get scattered. And meanwhile, the world seems to be coming unglued, for good. My daughter asked me if, as a young person, I had ever felt that the world was going haywire in dire and irreversible ways. No, was the correct answer, but I found the truth hard to utter to my child.

Our attentions seesaw from plane to plane, from issue to issue. The habit of forgetting, of compartmentalizing, is likely one of the oldest algorithms of the brain, derived from evolution: our biological ancestors, apes and cave creatures who could forget or compartmentalize each proximate disaster, were more likely to bring the necessary attention and focus to the business of survival. Did it help to know this fact? Maybe it did.

IN THE IMMEDIATE AFTERMATH of Dayana leaving, I did what needed to be done. I spread word far and wide for a caregiver for Mom. I wrote to all contacts who might be able to help. I employed social media. I called the local hospital and hospice. Within days I had people lined up for interviews. I met them in New Jersey. I met them in New York City. With some we Zoomed. Through the woman who babysat my children when they were young, I found Cynthia—a no-nonsense woman in her early seventies who has seen a thing or two, unflappable with eleven siblings of her own (she knows how to navigate turbulence), kind, game to help in all ways. She loves to garden.

My daughter went off to her senior year in college. Jasper, Mark, and I returned to New York City, visiting weekly to relieve Cynthia. The pandemic would recede, and my sisters would return. Time would carry us away from here, this part of the past.

* * *

THERE WAS SO MUCH I didn't know. I didn't know how long my mother would live, what would happen to the Farm, how I'd eventually crawl out of the depression. But I knew that Jasper would be fine, that I needed to be near him, that he was the only tree that mattered, and that I could stand, simply, facing the stove.

IT WOULD TAKE A second year for my saplings to grow above deer-grazing height, some getting as high as eight feet. I would lose only one or two more to the heat and dryness of summer 2022—the exact opposite of 2021, dry hot still days in which fires burned out of control in the forests of Greece, France, and Spain. Hottest summer ever recorded. By October most of my trees would be ready to move. I'd write to Duke and ask for his help. He'd come in his pickup with his shovel, planning to stay just a few minutes, assuming the trees wouldn't be viable for one reason or another. Most of his clients failed. Instead, we'd spend many hours digging up and moving the maple trees from the paddock to the Sandy Stand. Cynthia would help. My sister Laura would help, at the Farm for most of the fall to be near Mom and aid in her care. (Mark would be off canvassing for Fetterman in Pennsylvania, working to save democracy—otherwise he would have been there, too.)

Some of the hardest work I have ever done was bushwhacking through brambles, macheteing thickets and prickly shrubs to get the trees into the beautiful loamy soil. The trees were ready, tall, on their way to sleep for the winter, young still so their taproots had not yet formed. Duke looked up from a hole he was digging, caught my eye. "I don't mean to get spiritual," he said. "But this is the truth. There isn't anything better a person can do." The pessimistic forester wasn't a pessimist after all. And I hadn't failed.

A FROST IN LATE spring had killed my fig tree, but by summer it was sprouting again, and so were some of the ash stumps in the yard. A dead laurel tree near Sarah's cottage resurrected itself with an abundance of new growth. In the forest, I discovered that stumps from Dan the logger's handiwork were sprouting, too. Among these stumps were the stumps of a few tulip poplars (ones Dan swore to God and on the grave of his mother he hadn't cut) with shoots already a few feet high.

A raccoon found its way into the chicken coop and killed my flock, sixteen chickens and two roosters. Only one chicken survived the massacre, a Columbian Wyandotte, completely white with a spray of black feathers around her neck. We brought her to the house, set up a dog crate as her home. She sits on my mother's lap in the living room and patiently allows my mother to pet her.

A FEW YEARS BEFORE he died, Dan started his orchard—apples, plums, cherries, peaches. There was to be a tree for each one of us, even for the grandkids. After Dan died, my stepbrother Tony continued with the project for a while, until he, too, moved far away. Lying in the hammock in Dan's orchard—after a spring of cherries so abundant we had picked pounds of them and pitted them, and Mark made enough cherry pie filling to last a winter—I noticed an ugly fungus on every branch of the peach tree supporting one side of the hammock. It was called black knot and black knot spreads easily to neighboring fruit trees. Mark got out the chainsaw and cut the tree down. I bought an apricot tree to replace the dead peach. Livia wanted to add a pomegranate next. I wanted a persimmon.

Dan's vision, yes, but nobody owns the D chord or the G chord. And as Jung famously said, "I am not what happened to me, I am what I choose to become."

HERE IS ANOTHER GIFT, like a dream, the ever-present past: I am four years old. My sisters have been sent away for the summer, while I remain at home with my mother, too young to be sent off. My father has moved out. My mother and I spend long hours in bed, then in the kitchen or the garden or the yard. We sit with our backs resting against a soaring Liriodendron, shooting so high above us, its canopy like a huge umbrella protecting us from the heat of a summer day. The world is very slow. It is 1969. Men are about to land on the moon. It is just the two of us, my warm hand in hers, making plans for the long, long day that spreads out before us and into all other days.

Acknowledgments

Thank you to all my many siblings, a love beyond measure—Laura, Sarah, Jenny, Joan, Danny, Mary, Carrie, Hy, Tony, Cole, Andrew, Katherine, Vanessa. Thank you to Yolanda for her generosity, and to my father for his tireless guidance.

Thank you to my dear friends who have listened across the years—Wendy Amstutz, Christina Ball, Maria Campbell, Andrea Chapin, Elizabeth Gaffney, Jennifer Goodale, Kate Keenan, Année Kim, Sara Powers, Pamela Bol Riess, Elisabeth Schmitz, Cullen Stanley, Rene Steinke, Debbie Stier, Tracy Thorne, and Dodi Trotti.

Thank you to Sarah Poten, pandemic neighbor, garden mentor, beloved friend.

Thank you to Anthony, Brian, Dan, Duke, Tina, and D&R Greenway Land Trust for teaching me the beauty of forests.

Thank you, Lisa Herz, for helping me to see more clearly.

Acknowledgments

Thank you to Sally Howe, brilliant editor, and to Jin Auh and Sarah Chalfant, brilliant agents. Thank you to Scribner for ushering this book into the world, to the Wylie Agency, and to Hofstra University for their generous support.

Thank you to my mother, who gives love even now; to my children, who teach me daily and demand that I be brave; and thank you to Mark Svenvold, for everything—the magic sprinkled across my life.